A young Brando crossed with Bruce Lee

Strauchanie first rocked the football world when he was taken by Collingwood with their last draft pick in 2004. His efforts to get into the senior team have been chronicled on Channel 10's *Before the Game*.

Born in Horsham, Victoria, Bryan Strauchan now lives in Melbourne.

BRYAN STRAUCHAN

as told to Peter Helliar and Paul Calleja

My Story

The rise and rise of a genuine superstar of Australian sport

ALLEN&UNWIN

First published in 2007

Copyright © Peter Helliar and Paul Calleja 2007

All rights reserved. No part of this book may be reproduced or transmitted in any form or by any means, electronic or mechanical, including photocopying, recording or by any information storage and retrieval system, without prior permission in writing from the publisher. The *Australian Copyright Act 1968* (the Act) allows a maximum of one chapter or 10% of this book, whichever is the greater, to be photocopied by any educational institution for its educational purposes provided that the educational institution (or body that administers it) has given a remuneration notice to Copyright Agency Limited (CAL) under the Act.

Allen & Unwin
83 Alexander Street
Crows Nest NSW 2065
Australia
Phone: (61 2) 8425 0100
Fax: (61 2) 9906 2218
Email: info@allenandunwin.com
Web: www.allenandunwin.com

National Library of Australia
Cataloguing-in-Publication entry:

Helliar, Peter.
 Bryan Strauchan – my story: the rise and rise of a genuine superstar of Australian sport.
 1st ed.
 ISBN 9781741753431 (pbk.).
 1. Before the game (Television program). 2. Australian football players – Humor. 3. Australian football – Humor. 4. Australian wit and humor.   I. Calleja, Paul (Paul Anthony), 1963–. II. Title.
796.3360207

[handwritten annotation: It's my story, not his! Why is he before me?!?]

Cover designed by Studio Pazzo
Text designed by Pauline Haas
Typeset by Bluerinse Typesetting
Printed in Australia by McPherson's Printing Group

10 9 8 7 6 5 4 3 2 1

Dedicated to Bryan Keith Strauchan,
without whom none of this would be possible

contents

Preface ix
Foreword by Nathan Buckley xiii
Introduction xv

one	Roy of Horsham	1
two	China doll	15
three	Growing up Strauchanie	23
four	There is no 'I' in Strauchanie	35
five	Strauchanie rates his coaches	53
six	Me and Bucks	65
seven	That special boy	73
eight	Before Angelina …	85
nine	Strauchanie v Eddie	93
ten	Christi Almighty	101
eleven	A monument to the game	111
twelve	It's nice to be wanted	123
thirteen	The future of football	137
fourteen	Strauchanie speak	147
fifteen	Strauchanie's final words	155

Appendix 160
Bibliography 166
Acknowledgements 169
Index 172

preface

Strauchanie only reads books he writes so when the publisher approached him to write Volume One of his life story, he thought, better sooner than later. With nine Brownlows to come there will be a lot of volumes.

Anyway, once they sign you up the @#$%* publishers want everything. Family history, childhood stuff, whether I played well with others, early memories – how does anyone remember stuff like that? I reckon most people who write books make it up. So that's what Strachanie did. Until the @#$%* publishers got hold of my manuscript and started asking all these questions. Reminded me of school (see Chapter 3, Growing Up Strauchanie).

So, dear Fan of Strauchanie, you can see what I went through to tell you this inspiring story because I have left a lot of those queries in the book so you will know that it is all true, all checked, all verified, whatever they want to call it. They use words only Jimmy Clement would understand.

To give you an example of how difficult these people are to work with, here are some better titles Strauchanie came up with for this book that were all rejected by the publisher:

Strauchanie's Guide to the Galaxy
700 Saturdays
It's More Than a Boot
The Secret
The Third Testament
How Strauchanie Wins Friends and Influences People
Bryan Strauchan and the Deathly Hallows
Tuesdays With Strauchanie
The Sum of All Strauchanies
Clear and Present Strauchanie
Men Are From Mars, Strauchanie's From Venus
The Bridges of the Shire of Horsham
Strauchanie's Just Not That Into You
Who Moved Strauchanie's Cheese?
Memoirs of Strauchanie's Geisha

PREFACE

SYMBOLS USED

The good thing about being an elite AFL footballer is you are above the law and people adore you. This is not the case for most people. As a gesture of gratitude for buying Strauchanie's autobiography [although let's face it, you should be thanking me!] I have generously included pre-signed handwritten notes to get you out of almost any situation by adding a little bit of Strauchanie muscle. These are throughout the book and always have the 'bonus' symbol. Hirdy didn't put anything like this in his book so count yourselves lucky you didn't waste your money on that.

Psychic photos, like those ones in Harry Potter that wave, but even better because Strauchanie tells you what people were actually thinking when the photo was being taken.

No need for Strauchanie to blow his own trumpet when other people will blow it for him.

foreword

A word on BS from Nathan Buckley

I still vividly recall the first time I laid eyes on Bryan. He was head down and bum up, as always, looking for the full cream mayonnaise in the bottom drawer of the players' kitchen at the Lexus Centre. At that stage I wasn't aware of any new recruits and I was positive none of our players was wearing the number 59 jumper.

Needless to say, like Scott Burns on a hard ball get, he found the mayo and on turning around and seeing the puzzled look on my face all he said was: 'Strauchanieeee'.

Since that moment only one player at the club has shared a closer bond with BS than I have ... Jimmy Clement. Perhaps it was the way Jimmy opened his arms every time he saw Strauchanie walk through the double doors at Lexus. I can't be sure why, but their relationship has always left me with a tinge of jealousy. I still vividly recall the time when Strauchanie decided to accept Jimmy's offer of a lift [Strauchanie's always keen to save on petrol money] to a club function over mine. Strauchanie explained that he thought my car smelt of baby sick and that he would prefer to ride shotgun with Jimmy. It still surprises me how much that hurt.

Despite this, and the fact that Strauchanie probably feels I should have stood down to allow him to captain the club this year, we have become good mates both off the field and when he's not playing.

To be entirely honest, Strauchanie has provided a lot of balance for us at the club. While the rest of the playing list has focussed on a hardworking and team-oriented style of football, Strauchanie has always preached that the concept of the individual is bigger than the team. There is little doubt that he has lived it too. (Strauchanie has gone from an L to an XXL jumper with all his work in the players' kitchen.)

We all knew it was only a matter of time until Strauchanie would cash in and tell his inspirational story to provide himself with more money to maintain his high-flying C-list lifestyle.

I can honestly say there will never be another Strauchanie, and the boys at the club can't help but be thankful for that.

Nathan Buckley

introduction

The definition of irony: Strauchanie, the one man in Australia who needs no introduction, writing an introduction to his book. My publisher was adamant that I should introduce myself to anyone who hasn't yet heard of Bryan 'Strauchanie' Strauchan. Strauchanie still laughs at the notion of somebody not knowing who he is. Ha ha ha. If you haven't heard of me you've obviously been hiding under a rock, and if you're hiding under a rock, you're probably a terrorist, and Strauchanie would prefer it if you didn't read his book. The last thing Strauchanie needs is to be inspiring the wrong sorts of people.

Football has been a part of my life since the first time I knocked off a football from the local servo, aged six. I only got caught because a bloke with a neat haircut and a blue shirt and trousers spooked my dad, Roy Strauchan. 'Til this day, I still don't know why Dad freaked out so much, but he took off before young Strauchanie got back in the car. He was the one who sent me in there in the first place.

There I was, sitting behind the counter at the local servo in Horsham waiting for Dad to come back, having been busted for lifting a plastic footy, a carton of Camels and twenty-three Sherbet bombs. Little Strauchanie vowed then and there that he would never get caught with a footy in his hands ever again. Fast-forward eighteen years, and defenders still shake their heads in wonderment at how this sporting superstar, with the movie star good looks and the rock star attitude, has made such an impact in such little time. In the world of AFL football the term 'superstar' is bandied around far too easily for Strauchanie's liking. I once overheard Steve Quartermain refer to Essendon's James Hird as a 'superstar' at a Channel 10 Christmas party. Strauchanie unwound on an unsuspecting Quarters, 'Call yourself a commentator! James Hird a superstar? Come off it! Tell him to win a Brownlow and then come talk to me!' Quarters tried to tell me that Hirdy had, in fact, won the coveted medal a few years ago. But by the time he could say 'See the Bombers fly up' Strauchanie had already moved on and was having a crack at an ex-Big Brother housemate Not entirely sure which one, they all look the same to me [but not in a racist way].

People often approach me in the street and say, 'Strauchanie, you are a superstar'. I say 'thanks' because dealing with the public is just as much a part of being an AFL footballer as kicking goals or turning up to training, although sometimes, I have to remind coach Mick Malthouse of this football reality. He twitches his mo and walks off remaining unconvinced. Bobby Skilton who, as his name suggests, had a ton of skill, took Strauchanie aside once and had a word. He said, 'Strauchanie, I won three Brownlows' [I went along with his fantasy of three Brownlows because the old bugger was a little tipsy] but I have never seen a player take this entire sport to a new level like you have, Strauchanie'. I looked at Bobby, a little confused: how could a bloke who has deluded himself into thinking he has won, not one, not two, but three Brownlows, be so spot on in his assessment of Strauchanie? I explained to Bobby that it all comes down to heritage. My mother is Chinese and my dad is from Horsham, which equals perfect football pedigree. Strauchanie has the aerial grace of a Shaolin Monk crossed with the ability to give you a roundhouse from behind if you're getting on top at the stoppages.

I will always be grateful for the opportunity I have been given by the Collingwood Football Club. I will never forget D-Day – Draft Day. Strauchanie sat with Dad (Roy) and Mum (Soy Bean) glued to the telly. Strauchanie's folks were as proud as punch. Dad with his Bulldogs scarf and Mum with her apron still on, after whipping up a batch of Fortune Cookies with each one saying 'Western Bulldogs'. They were so happy for Strauchanie until, that is, Neil Balme read out 'Bryan Strauchan' and drove the proverbial chopstick through Mum's heart. Dad was upset, but after so many strokes [47 in 1996 alone], he struggled to show as much emotion as Mum. It didn't worry Strauchanie, to be honest, because Strauchanie knew that if you want to be a true superstar then you have to get to the Lexus Centre, and that's exactly where I headed . . . in my ~~Ford~~ Cortina.

Sure there have been ups and downs. Finding out I was adopted, breaking Christi Malthouse's heart, Christi breaking Strauchanie's heart, getting my first game, getting locked in the stairwell at Telstra Stadium before my first game and, of course, winning nine consecutive Brownlow medals from 2007–2015.

So buckle up and get ready for a bumpy ride, it's Yum Cha Time!!

#59

Bryan 'Superstar' Strauchan

I include evidence of how my publisher tried to censor me, but Strauchanie threatened to stop working on the book — whose story is it??

Bryan,

As discussed in our last phone call, a thorough read of your resubmitted manuscript has indicated that many of your facts still need verifying.

I have listed below some of our major concerns, as well as marking up instances on the attached pages.

PAGE 6: lines 5–6

Please stop dressing predictions as fact. At the time of publishing you are still yet to play a game in the 2007 season.

Bet you feel silly about this one now!!
– BS

CHAPTER ONE→

one

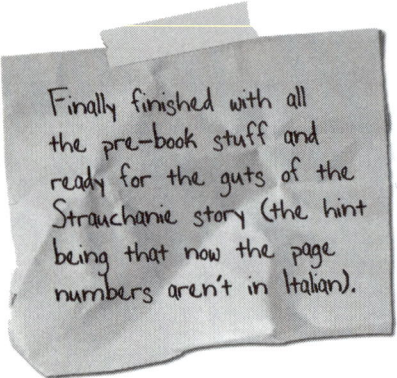

Finally finished with all the pre-book stuff and ready for the guts of the Strauchanie story (the hint being that now the page numbers aren't in Italian).

The publisher asked Strauchanie to start at the beginning of his family history so the readers could see his origins as a superstar. It wasn't easy getting the story out of Mum and Dad but this is what I've come up with. And Strauchanie agrees it was worth doing because of his unusual cultural heritage. His story is an important part of Australian history.

Don't ever tell Roy Strauchan unco boys can't play sport. They tried in 1959 and they failed. The Government, local councils, sporting clubs, parents of unco children. Roy Strauchan never listened. He refused to conform to popular beliefs and as a result, the final of the Horsham Primary Grade Three 50-metre sprint was won by Brett 'Spazz' Dooley. It was Roy's [or Dad, as I liked to call him] proudest moment. Sure, Spazz Dooley was given a 10-metre head start before it ended in a controversial photo finish [remembering this was years before mobile phones were invented, so Strauchanie has no idea what they used for cameras] but the point was made, and the excitement at seeing Spazz wobble over the finish line was palpable.

My dad was born in 1930, the same year that Phar Lap won the Melbourne Cup, and in the midst of the Great Depression. I've often laughed with Dad that it was fair enough that he had to live through the Depression, considering there was so much unbridled joy to follow, in years to come, with the arrival of a baby boy that would turn the football and entertainment world on its ear [that's me if you haven't picked it up yet: Strauchanie!!].

Dad was born to my grandparents, Ernest and Betty Strauchan. Ernest was a self-made man, not literally of course, making his money in IT after the Great War. Personally, Strauchanie doesn't see what was so 'great' about the war or the Depression and if it was so 'great' then quit complaining about it because, at the end of the day, Strauchanie doesn't give a flying toss how far you had to walk to school. Ernest was Ernest by name and earnest by nature. He called a spade a spade but not in a racist way. He was the first person to use the term 'softknob'. Ernest instilled into my father the work ethic of a Clydesdale. Strangely enough, Dad also inherited Ernest's hairy feet and bad breath. Ernest could be heard boasting, at the local Twig and Berries Hotel, that he once fought Ned Kelly in a cage match, and had him in a headlock so tight, that Ned walked away swearing never to let any man get him in a headlock ever again.

Grandma Betty was born in a quaint little B&B in Daylesford, Victoria, a town famous for its hot springs and lesbians. Betty was proudly bi-curious, and Strauchanie once found an entry in her diary which referred to a three-way, involving two members of the Kelly Gang [which lead to the cage match with a jealous Ernest Strauchan]. The three-way was the Thursday before the Glenrowan siege, and Betty recounted in the pages of her diary how the two members of the Kelly Gang, Dan and Ned, made her feel like a woman. The episode made the papers all the way down to Bairnsdale, with the revered Bairnsdale Enquirer running with the front page headline, 'Floozy Not So Choosy'. Ned Kelly was hung in the Melbourne Gaol soon after, but only Nanna Betty knew how hung he really was.

Betty was known for her flirtatious dress sense [not unlike Strauchanie who stole the Brownlow show last year with a beautiful oriental vest. It was so sharp it took the spotlight away from Rebecca Twigley's cleavage. The AFL has since apologised for having a special 'cleavage spotlight' and has vowed not to use it again]. Betty regularly wore her Sunday dress inches above her ankles. In 1928 she became the first woman in the world to wear trousers. For this she was sentenced to death by firing squad, only to successfully appeal the decision. But that did not endear her to the local mob, who, without a game show to provide an outlet, were hungry for a lynching and they clearly did not understand Nanna Betty's lifestyle choices. When a mob gets confused, they get angry real quick and the mob was angry, like the time Collingwood tried to introduce a dress code for the cheer squad. Strauchanie had to step in and explain to the board that some of these people didn't own jeans or collared shirts and it could cause disharmony. The board relented and the cheer squad has remained as underdressed as ever. But the mob was angry at Betty, not only because of their views of what should be allowed to go on between a lady and a woman but also because, on that particular day, a total fire ban was in force, meaning that the angry mob could not light their firesticks. Although this mob wanted mob justice, it wasn't going to test the boundaries of the law to get it. Disappointed with not having proper mob firesticks, the mob politely asked Betty to leave town. Betty may have been wearing trousers but she was nothing, if not a lady. She calmly gathered a turtle neck and a case of soap and left Daylesford forever. She walked tall, proudly displaying the famous Strauchanie wit on the way out: 'I guess now I'm Goodbye Bye-Curious'. The joke was lost on the toothless mob and so was Nanna Betty.

> PAGE 11:
> Bryan, something is not right here. The Kelly Gang incident actually happened in 1880, so this would have to have happened *before* Betty puts on trousers in Daylesford in 1928. But in this story, Ernest fights Ned Kelly (in 1880?), jealous over the Kelly Gang affair. But Betty doesn't meet Ernest until 1928. Bryan, are you sure you have your facts right?
>
> Yep – all rechecked + correct – BS

BRYAN STRAUCHAN: MY STORY

With nothing but an image of a former lover etched into her brain, a turtle neck so ahead of its time it was considered space-age and a block of lavender soap that made her smell of the colour purple, Betty landed in Ballarat. It was here that Nanna Betty first laid eyes on Grandad Ernest who was in town for a seminar on a new product called Windows '29. It was set to revolutionise the printing press, as it carried an exciting new font called 'Times New Roman'. After a hard day learning the new system, Ernest dropped into the local watering hole for a pint or two of brew. It was here that Ernest Strauchan and Betty Phillips were embroiled in one of Ballarat's biggest scandals, something that their future superstar grandson would be no stranger to. It was also where Ernest and Betty would fall in love.

Ernest had been attentive during the Windows '29 lecture. He had taken plenty of notes, most of them making sense, while occasionally drifting off and doodling a caricature of a naked woman or his own genitals [an offence that carried the punishment of five years solitary confinement]. He sat next to a likeable local named Clancy Kane. Ernest and Clancy got along like a pyromaniac's house on fire. Swapping recipes for damper and comparing beards during lunch breaks, it wasn't until Clancy dropped into the local to let Ernest know his own beard had grown half an inch since lunch, that all hell broke loose. Ernest, being a generous sort of fella, offered Clancy a round of beer [Strauchanie is the most generous bloke down at Collingwood, although sometimes I wonder if it's all worth it. Once I lent Scott

Am no longer prepared to argue Windows '29 with you. Please check your facts, Bryan.

Pendlebury two dollars for a packet of Pretzels and I haven't seen it since]. Clancy, being a renowned tightarse, accepted, even requesting that a packet of potato chips and fried calamari rings be added to the deal.

Ernest, rarely seen on the back foot, accepted reluctantly. Now, Clancy may have had a tight arse, but he had the bladder of a 93-year-old woman. After three sips of his stout, Clancy decided he needed to pay a visit to the gents. Feeling comfortable enough to peer through his new found friend's notes from the class, what Ernest saw was disturbing. Not only did he see his exact same notes scribbled on Clancy's page, but he also saw his own genitals staring back at him. Ernest was furious. They were called private parts for a reason. The Ballarat stranger, who had sat next to him, was no longer a friend. He was a copycat. Besides terrorists and religious figures, Ernest hated nothing more than copycats, and this copycat from Ballarat was the worst he had ever seen. [Strauchanie hates copycats too. Have spoken to Dale Thomas about that.] As Clancy re-entered the bar, advising everyone to allow ten minutes for the smallest room in the house to regather itself and freshen up, Ernest let burst with a tirade not seen in Ballarat since a woodchopper's axe was found to be made in Taiwan. He became a ravenous dog fighting for his bone, a lion protecting its young, a Bulldogs cheer squad member preparing to go into battle for his teeth. 'No-one doodles my doodle but me, you hear me Clancy Kane!' His words pierced the room. Nobody risked speaking, fearing their words would carry fateful consequences. The bar fell silent, as if Julie Anthony had walked into the room to sing the National Anthem. Outside, people gathered as the rumour of the impending dust-up swept through the main street and into the salons and shoe shops of the bustling promenade. 'These are my balls!' Ernest roared.

Clancy swallowed hard, the weight of the situation arriving on his shoulders like a 747, which at the time was just a series of numbers and not a massive commercial aircraft. 'Don't be daft,' muttered the tightarse, 'they could be anyone's balls ...' BANG! The next sound sent a ripple through the air that could be felt in Sunbury. Gasp after gasp could be heard, like a barbershop quartet in desperate need of a Fisherman's Friend. Then, relief. The sound was not a bang. It was actually a THUD! The thud was the sound of Ernest Strauchan's belt buckle hitting the ground, like a stroke victim falling off a horse. There he stood, Ernest Strauchan, self-made man, standing in the most crowded room in Ballarat, naked from the waist down. Strangely, a lacy pair of knickers were now residing around his knees. It was later revealed that old Ernie had performed the horizontal La Bamba with the Windows '29 tutor, Miss Audrey Garrison. She protested the injustice of the revelation, however her words fell on deaf ears because right now nobody cared that the hardest man in town was wearing frilly panties, like a hammock around his tree trunk legs. It was what was swinging between those trees that had everybody aghast. Nobody knew where to look. Somebody needed to speak, to say something to help cure this situation of its awkwardness. Betty Phillips was that somebody. She spoke up like Mick Malthouse rallying the troops [this was after Strauchanie's practical joke of peeing in the urn at half-time on Anzac Day had everybody a little frazzled, especially when Scotty Burns went to enjoy his post-game cuppa]. Betty recommended Clancy Kane receive the strap for his copycat ways and that the town not bury this historical moment like they had buried the memory of the infamous persecution in 1906 of redheads and left-handed batsmen. 'We should celebrate this moment,' she insisted. There was a general murmur from the stunned crowd, who were still ushering their eyes to safe areas of the hotel. 'But how should we commemorate such an occasion?' they asked in unison, as if it had been choreographed in a musical. 'By putting it in a child's rhyme,' she responded. A dissident in the shape of Miss Garrison spoke up. 'It still isn't fair, after all, I did lose my underwear!' Betty quickly responded, 'Oh shut up, tramp, you'll get a mention.' At that moment, Ernest Strauchan knew two things. One, he was going to marry that woman, and two, it was time to pull up his pants ... temporarily.

For the next week, Ernie Strauchan and Betty Phillips made love so passionately and loudly that by the Wednesday a curfew had been enforced. Their love-making sessions went on for hours, interrupted only by a lunch break, a couple of drinks breaks and one for tea, but then it was back to the love-making. And it was love. It wasn't banging or nailing or screwing, in fact, it had nothing at all to do with hardware, it was all about love. On that night, in a ramshackle shed [albeit with WIRs] Betty Phillips fell pregnant and Ernest fell for Betty. They married the following Tuesday in a ceremony reported as 'lovely and event free'. They honeymooned in Horsham, and they never left.

Roy Strauchan, like his father Ernest, became a hard man. He once claimed he was the only man to be born with pubic hair. He had a passion for sport that was surpassed only by his complete inability to play any kind of sport successfully [something not passed down to his superstar son, thankfully]. Simply, he was the most uncoordinated man ever to walk down the main street of Horsham. He once rode a bike into a wishing well and stayed trapped for two-and-a-half days, surviving only on head lice and sherbert bombs. God may not have blessed Roy with an abundance of sporting talent, but he did give him a generous helping of determination. He once sprained an ankle during a spelling bee, but fought on, only to spell the word 'persistent' incorrectly and finish second to Brett Dooley Senior. He once nearly bled to death after attempting to remove a safety pin from a tag that was left over from the drycleaners. On another occasion he pierced his 'lollybag' with an occy strap, trying to pack the boot for a weekend away at Rosebud. The doctor said it was the worst scrotum injury he had ever seen and was ever likely to see. Upon recovery, the doctor told Roy he would never have kids. Roy laughed, not surprisingly, considering he was on the gas at the time. He was also laughing because that was the only way he could react. Nobody ever told Roy Strauchan what to do. If you told Roy to turn hard left, he would only veer left. If you told him something was black, he would say it was a dark brown. If you told him to jump off the West Gate Bridge, he would jump off the Murray Creek Bridge. He was always just a little bit different. [Strauchanie's a bit similar. Mick once told me to play full-back in a scratch match against the Roos, Strauchanie settled himself at full-forward. We got beaten by nineteen goals. Not Strauchanie's fault if the backs won't man up.]

(legs)

Roy never let his unco-ness get in the way of him enjoying his sport. His results were improving too. He ran the 100 metres in under thirty seconds, he made a convincing twelve in a cricket final and was promoted to wing attack for the local mixed netball team, the Late Bloomers. Roy believed in himself, perhaps too much, many thought. His grade five teacher, Russell Harrison-Smith-Peterson-Clarke, explained: 'Every question I asked in class, Roy was always the first to raise his hand, and every time he got the question wrong. For a while I banned the raising of hands, then I banned all questions, then I banned Roy. Not overtly, but I would send him on errands. I would send him to the Staff Room to get a piece of yellow chalk or I would send him to the pharmacist to get some dingers. Anything to get him out of the classroom. When he left, I would furiously begin teaching the other students. They would scurry for knowledge like seagulls, but when he got back, they knew it was heads on desk for a bit of nap time. Sometimes we would wait for Roy to fall asleep and then carry on with the lesson in mime.

Don't get me wrong, he tried hard, bloody hard but he just wasn't very bright'. [Sometimes Strauchanie feels embarrassed about being such a culture-vulture in front of Dad, but the fact is that Strauchanie is one sophisticated mofo.]

After Roy failed his final year of school, for the seventh time in a row, the State Government granted special permission for Horsham High to allow Roy to pass under special consideration. In 1957 Roy Strauchan graduated from high school, aged twenty-seven and as proud as a hubcap. As unqualified as a beanie auditioning for the role of Macbeth, Roy Strauchan auditioned for the role of Macbeth at the Horsham Performing Arts Centre, where he was told by the theatre director, Todd Armstrong, that he 'would rather have a beanie play Macbeth than give him the role'. With no university prepared to accept him and no trade willing to take a risk on him, Roy took on the only job he felt a passion for: special PE teacher at Horsham High. The staff were nervous about hiring Roy, but after nine PE teachers had been involved in a Big Lunch cockfighting ring behind the shelter-sheds, the faculty believed hiring the town's favourite simpleton could be a good PR move. He would have nothing to do with the First 18 or the First 11. He would be in charge of 'the sportingly challenged' students – those whose motor skills were limited to changing the colour on a multicoloured biro. It was here where Roy found true happiness, his reason for being, the key to his place in the world.

Whether it was teaching an agoraphobic how to serve and volley or showing Amanda Sockworthy how to skip through a rope without having a panic attack, Roy

ROY OF HORSHAM

got the best out of people, even if his methods were unorthodox. He once made his entire class run the 400 metres with pieces of Lego in their shoes. Another time he threatened a member of the SRC with a javelin if he did not throw a shot-put more than six metres. He once kicked a water-logged ball into the face of an exchange student so hard he had to go home to Argentina for facial correction surgery. Why he did it was never revealed. The only thing Roy said at the time was that the matter was between 'Miguel and me'. Many were shocked at Roy's behaviour, as a bloodied and screaming Miguel, disorientated, made his way to the First Aid room with Roy, at close range, yelling at the top of his lungs, 'Oh, what's the matter? Oh, don't cry for me, Argentina.' Roy was given a suspended sentence of two weeks for this incident, and was given yard duty for the following month. [This is probably where Strauchanie got his love of the sledge. During a practice match against the Dockers, Strauchanie let rip at Des Headland:

13
Dale...
unlucky!

Strauchanie, aged 6 months

You †%$#‡ ##$% and | @‡ $% ##$% †-ing if you ##@† *#% think again ^$†$#!@ biatch!

The publisher believed this statement to be inappropriate and it has since been censored under the AFL's new code of conduct policies.

Strauchanie has inherited Dad's love of teaching. I once took Dids aside and tried to teach him how to kick more accurately. He swore in Croatian and ran off. Strauchanie reckons if you're going to have a go at someone, at least have the decency to have a go at them in their own language, otherwise it just comes across as a little bit racist.

14
Wakes me up before you go go! lol

Despite the occasional rap across the knuckles from the 'suits in the staff room', Roy loved teaching unco kids physical education. He was at his happiest with a polo shirt, a whistle and a sun visor. Little did he know that he had only scratched the surface when it came to true happiness, which was, as it turns out, heading to Horsham, all the way from China.

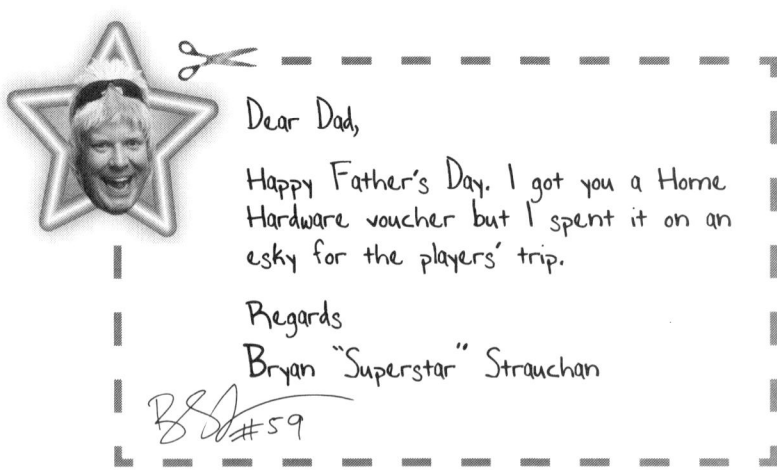

Dear Dad,

Happy Father's Day. I got you a Home Hardware voucher but I spent it on an esky for the players' trip.

Regards
Bryan "Superstar" Strauchan
BS #59

two

Bryan, please see the query on page 18

My mother is proudly Asian. Not just because being Asian has become trendy since the success of *Shanghai Noon*, but because she was born in China, which is considered the Asianist country of them all. Born in a village outside Fujin, in the north/south of the country, Soy Bean Xinag had what is known as a 'regulation birth', which, in China, means she was born with dark straight hair, before many photographs were taken. Her parents, whose names Strauchanie has never been able to pronounce, were supposedly proud people with a passion for the martial arts, kung-fu movies and Bruce Lee. Strauchanie's grandfather, whose name sounded like a fabric softener to Strauchanie, designed the Great Wall of China. Originally, it was going to be a cyclone fence, until Grandfather stepped up at a meeting in Saigon and spoke up. It was his proudest achievement. [He didn't actually build the wall, he was not prone to heavy lifting. Probably where Strauchanie got his famous work ethic from.]

**Bryan, Saigon is in Vietnam. Please get the story straight.

CHINA DOLL

Grandfather met Grandmother over a cup of noodles at a Bruce Lee festival in Xilinji. After a romantic night enjoying *Way of the Dragon*, Grandfather put his arm around Grandmother and said 'Let me show you the way of my dragon'. [Grandfathers metaphoric use of the film title *Enter the Dragon* was deemed unprintable by the publisher of this book.] However, Grandmother was not as easy as the chicks in the Collingwood cheer squad. She needed some extra convincing and Grandfather was up to the task commenting, 'You know the Great Wall isn't the only thing you can see from outer space', before unzipping his pleated trousers and kicking off his slippers. They made love under the Chinese sky before cooking up some Chinese food [known in China simply as 'food'] and taking photos of each other in the nude. Those photos remained private for many years until a neighbour found them and posted them on the Internet in 1999, receiving more than six thousand hits.

Grandfather was executed in 1952, after speaking out against the Chinese government's policies, especially the one which banned the broadcasting of the hit American television shows *Mister Ed* and *Leave it to Beaver*. The

Dear Grandma,

Sorry to hear about Pop ... you'll live.

Regards
#59 Bryan "Superstar" Strauchan

Chinese government believed the idea of a talking horse was demonic, and that *Leave it to Beaver* was too sexually suggestive, despite nobody from the CCC (the Chinese Censorship Committee) ever seeing it. Countrymen lived in fear of the communist regime, but Grandfather always stood up for what he believed in. Grandfather came from a proud line of Chinese men, his family could be traced all the way back to the Han Dynasty [no relation to Mitchell Hahn from the Bulldogs] yet suddenly he was as dead as a corked thigh, just because he tried to organise a working bee in Shanghai to raise money for a megaphone to be used for speaking out against the government. Grandmother hid in the hills in the north, mourning the loss of her husband and 'the best root of her life'. Her pain was eased somewhat by the fact that she was pregnant with child. While her country was at war, inside her belly hope blossomed in the form of the most beautiful foetus Asia had ever ultrasounded. There was so much uncertainty facing Grandmother, she was only sure of two things: one, this baby would be strong and, two, it would not be born in China. She hitched the first donkey out of that two-bit mountain enclave and headed for the bright lights of Vietnam, whose future looked so shiny the Emperor was forced to wear shades. It was 1960.

Not long after Grandmother arrived in Vietnam, so did many Americans and they stayed a long time. This is when

> PAGES 16 & 18:
> Bryan, p. 18 you say that Grandmother was determined her daughter NOT be born in China but on page 16 you say Soy Bean was born in China. What is the real story?

Strauchanie = international man of mystery

CHINA DOLL

Grandmother showed early signs of the genes that would one day create a sporting superstar when she got a job at a bar playing ping-pong and darts [unfortunately, no photos exist of Grandmother playing such sports]. Grandmother lived in Vietnam with her newborn daughter, Soy Bean, for fifteen years and left in 1975, after the fall of Saigon. She knew a better life lay elsewhere. Not exactly sure where that life lay, Grandmother spent a couple of yen at the local movie house where a new film from Australia was playing. That film was *Alvin Purple* [released in China under the title *Sexy Sexy Sex Man*] and that classic movie changed all of our lives. Grandmother booked two tickets to Australia and said goodbye to Saigon.

It is often said, where I grew up, that the fall of Saigon lead directly to the rise of Horsham. Grandmother lived in Drung South, 25 kilometres from Horsham, with her growing daughter Soy Bean for all too few years before dying in a tragic shoelace-tying accident. [It's still too emotional for the Strauchans to talk about, but let's just say I'm always a little nervous whenever I loop the loop and I'll never do a double-back lace for as long as I live.] Soy Bean, orphaned at the age of twenty-nine, began working as a lollipop lady. After nine children were seriously injured, on nine different occasions, Soy Bean took some unpaid leave and travelled to Horsham to try to trap a man. Her plan was to fall pregnant to this man and never work again. That man ended up being Roy Strauchan, who had hands the size of pineapples and just as rough. You knew when you had been felt up by Roy Strauchan, which resulted in quite a few sexual harassment

LEMON CHICKEN

Serves 4 (or 1 if Strauchanie's eating)

This is Strauchanie's favourite meal as cooked by my mum. My dad would always say, 'Why would you pay big bucks to go to the Flower Drum when there's a magnificent lemon chicken right here, with the chance for a bit of slap and tickle after dinner as well?'

Ingredients

- 5 teaspoons cornflour (it's not advised to eat cornflour straight out of the packet as Strauchanie discovered)
- ½ cup chicken stock
- 1 lemon, rind finely grated, juiced
- 1½ tablespoons caster sugar
- 2 teaspoons soy sauce (usually you'll find enough at the bottom of a used dim sim bag)
- 1 garlic clove, crushed (like Strauchanie's heart after Christi left me)
- 2 eggwhites
- canola oil, for deep-frying
- 600 g chicken breast fillets, cut into 1 cm-thick strips (try not to giggle when saying the word 'breast')
- 6 green onions, sliced
- lemon wedges, to serve

CHINA DOLL

FYI: Number of recipes in Hirdy's book = 0

Method

1. Blend 1½ teaspoons cornflour with 1 tablespoon of stock until smooth (as Strauchanie's kicking action). Add remaining stock, lemon rind, lemon juice, sugar, soy sauce and garlic. Pour lemon mixture into a wok. Cook over medium heat for 4 minutes or until mixture comes to the boil (like Mick when we're 5 goals down at half-time). Set aside.

2. Whisk eggwhites in a bowl until frothy (Dale Thomas uses this solution in his hair). Whisk in remaining cornflour.

3. Pour oil into a large saucepan until it is one-third full. Heat over medium-high heat until hot. Dip one-third of chicken strips into eggwhite mixture. Lower into oil. Cook for 1 to 2 minutes or until golden and cooked through. Drain on paper towels (or on Mike Sheehan's Top 50 article). Keep warm. Repeat twice with remaining chicken and eggwhite mixture.

4. Return sauce to stovetop over medium heat. Cook, stirring, for 3 minutes (as you do to Fraser Gehrig to put him off his game) or until heated through. Stir through onions. Place chicken into a serving dish. Pour over sauce. Scoff down like there's no tomorrow.

Enjoy – BS

complaints in the Horsham High staff room. Fortunately for Dad, sexual harassment hadn't been invented at that stage, so his groping antics were, if not enjoyed, then tolerated.

It was at the local watering hole where Dad and Mum first met. Strauchanie's never been told the full story but in short, Dad was half-cut and Mum was bang up for it. Dad, always thinking on his feet, swept Mum up [Mum couldn't walk at this stage after her ninth Sambuca] and took Mum to his office in the high school gym. That night Roy Strauchan lay Soy Bean down on the official high school high jump mat, and they made love in a way that made the cyclone-fencing walls of Dad's office shake, then blush with envy. Dad had never made much of a splash in the pool, but that night he had a relay team of swimmers heading straight towards Mum's ovaries with one mission: to create a sporting superstar. It is fitting that Strauchanie was conceived with so much sporting equipment looking down upon the act: T.W. Sherrins, Gray-Nicholls, Spalding 7-irons, Wilson racquets, all giving their blessing to this soon-to-be superhuman.

Thirteen months later, Strauchanie was born, after a birth that was described as 'painful as all *%$#'. Around the streets of Horsham, local legend has it that Strauchanie wasn't born on a gym mat, it was a manger and by Christ, it may have just been true.

PAGE 22:
Bryan, something doesn't add up here. Soy Bean was born in 1960 (see page 18). She's orphaned at 29, making it 1989. That means you were born after 1989, making you 18 at time of publication.

Huh? My Lemon Chicken recipe should have cleared this up for you.

CHAPTER THREE→

GROWING UP STRAUCHANIE

three

My only criticism of the Bible is that there are very few references to Jesus as a youngster. Why don't we hear about teenage Jesus? Was he always in time-out? What kind of kid was he in the playground? Did he share his little lunch with the poor kids who could only afford brand-free cheese puffs and dry biscuits? Or did he feed his classmates loaves and fishes every Big Lunch? Did he make the local football team? Where did he play? Was he a flashy forward, capable of kicking a miracle goal, but guilty of going missing? Or was he a rugged half-back flanker who provided direction, a spiritual leader? Did he get favourable treatment from the umps because he was the Son of God or was he [metaphorically] crucified?

When Strauchanie agreed to write this book he wanted to make sure of one thing – he wouldn't make the same mistakes the Bible did. So I've included a 'behind the shelter-sheds' look at how a superstar grew up.

GROWING UP STRAUCHANIE

Strauchanie has been special from a very early age. Somehow I was born with a sense of the importance of breastfeeding as a means of gaining essential nutrients. I was so up for breastfeeding that it got to the point where I'd just latch on to whichever woman happened to be walking past. Sometimes it was easier for Mum just to give me to Uncle Troy. His man boobs would keep me occupied for at least ten to fifteen minutes. But then before too long, Mum had put a pie in the blender and baby Strauchanie's on to solids.

Mum would get embarrassed when she took me to the maternal health centre. I was just so far ahead of the other kids in almost every category. The longest baby – Strauchanie. The heaviest baby – Strauchanie. The baby with the biggest head – Strauchanie. The baby with the straightest projectile vomit – Strauchanie [probably where Strauchanie gets his 'deadeye dick' accuracy from in front of the big sticks!] Mum knew, there and then, that there was something different about this little boy and without hesitation she entered me into the shopping centre baby competition circuit.

In typical Strauchanie fashion, my first appearance created big waves. As soon as they laid eyes on baby Strauchanie, the other mums started to panic. I had them worried all right, and the dirty tricks campaign was underway immediately. It began when they started questioning my eligibility. 'That baby's huge', one mum quipped. 'There's no way he's in the one-to-two-year-old category!' Mum was eventually forced to produce my birth certificate. Another mum then complained that I was a health and safety risk, in that I might roll over and squash her kid. Please! You've seen Strauchanie weave his way out of a pack. I was born with the awareness of where people are around me. The organisers even received an anonymous tip-off that I was a dwarf dressed up as a kid. Mum was in tears the day she found out that someone had suggested that I be subjected to a DNA test to prove that I did not suffer from dwarfism. In the end, it wasn't worth the trouble. Little Roxy Marlowe would always win anyway. Sure, she looked cute, but it came as no surprise to me when it was later revealed that her win-at-all-costs mother, had paid for her to have plastic surgery at the age of 18 months. Eventually, Mum thought, enough was enough and she withdrew me from the competition. Just in time, I might add. I was on my last warning for rolling over and squashing the Furlong twins, when, on my way out, I accidentally stood on Roxy Marlowe's floor-length hair, ripping out her $400 hair extensions. It ruined her chances that day, prompting even an infant Strauchanie to raise his chubby little arms in the air and yell, 'Strauchanie!' in baby talk.

Young Strauchanie, aged 18 months

    School didn't get off to the best start for Strauchanie. I wet myself on the first day. Wet myself again on the second day. On the third day I managed to wet myself, Josh Gregson and Mrs Devenport, my teacher. Some of the kids cruelly dubbed me Bryan 'Pissy Pants' Strauchan or 'PP' for short. Luckily, I was tough enough to deal with it and clever enough to draw attention away from myself by making fun of Dennis 'Hole in the Heart' Modlington. I eventually grew out of the wetting myself phase and have only had a couple of recurrences since. Last year's Copeland Trophy night being one of them, although I still maintain that I passed out and that Dale Thomas tipped a bottle of beer down the front of my pants. I had to go outside the casino, take my pants off

BRYAN STRAUCHAN: MY STORY

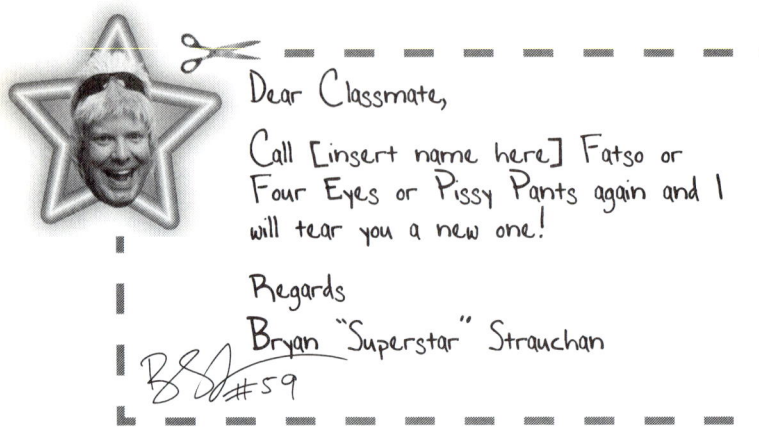

Dear Classmate,

Call [insert name here] Fatso or Four Eyes or Pissy Pants again and I will tear you a new one!

Regards
Bryan "Superstar" Strauchan
BS #59

and hold them up to one of the fireball towers, in an attempt to dry them. I swear I heard someone from the gathered crowd call out, 'Hey, look, it's Pissy Pants Strauchan!'

Secondary school brought its own challenges. Historically, most people with extraordinary talent struggle to fit into the mainstream system. Strauchanie was no exception. The school didn't cater for me academically. How am I supposed to excel if I'm in veggie Maths, veggie English and veggie Home Ec? Fortunately, I had already decided that I was going to be an AFL footballer and that an education wasn't necessary. If I'd been allowed to study future-telling like at Hogwarts, I would have got A/A++

> Strauchanie would be in the top 40 hardest workers down at the club... top 70 if you include the guys and girls in admin.
> PAUL LICURIA

There was, however, one reason I stayed on to complete my schooling and that was the love of my life [BC – Before Christi]. Her name – Linda Fratelli.

I was in Year 8 when the word got around that a new girl had started that day. 'Hot' was the word being 'Daniel' bandied around [Strauchanie can't help himself being clever with players' names] and Strauchanie couldn't wait to see what all the fuss was about. Recess came and a few of us were playing kick to kick in the quadrangle. Strauchanie temporarily forgot we were on asphalt and paid dearly after taking a sliding chest mark on his knees. The next thing you know, Craig Dyson elbows me in the ribs, points to the stairs and whispers, 'There she is.' I look up, and there, before my very eyes, coming down the stairs, seemingly in slow motion and with her long dark brown hair flowing in the breeze, is the most beautiful girl Strauchanie had ever set eyes upon – Linda Fratelli. Flanked by two friends, she turns to one of them and smiles. This isn't just any smile. This is a mesmerising smile that sends out a wave of captivation that stops every boy in his tracks. The football fell from my limp hands, the nearby game of foursquare came to an abrupt halt and Mark Bentley stopped halfway up the flagpole on his way to retrieve his PE shorts. This girl was stunning beyond belief, and she was now heading Strauchanie's way. Thinking quickly, I told Craig to kick the ball in her direction. He did. Strauchanie then took off, watching the ball in flight, while, at the same time, thinking to himself, this is going to land right next to ... 'BANG! Oops, I've just bowled someone over.' I looked down. Uh-oh, it was Linda. She

BRYAN STRAUCHAN: MY STORY

HORSHAM EAST SECONDARY COLLEGE

MID-YEAR REPORT 1998

STUDENT: BRYAN STRAUCHAN
HOMEROOM: 9 Purple

MATHEMATICS *Mr P. Grundy*
Bryan's obsession with the 'boobs' gag on the calculator is pathetic. His classmates are so sick of it that they've taken to hiding his calculator. His exam result is the lowest on record, with him only answering one question in the geometry section, that being: Describe a cube. Bryan's answer: A word that rhymes with boob.
GRADE: E

SCIENCE *Mrs M. McNaffy*
Bryan's complete lack of adherence to the safety rules in the laboratory was evident when he used the Bunsen burner to light one of his rectal emissions. The resultant flame melted three ribs on our plastic skeleton and scorched the eyebrows of another student. He also turned our rat dissection lesson into a farce by using a pizza slicer as a cutting device.
GRADE: E

ITALIAN *Ms L. Donato*
Bryan's belief that he has already mastered the Italian language has severely hindered his progress. I'm constantly explaining to Bryan that the Italian language isn't just English words with the letters 'a' on the end of them, but Bryan is convinced 'thata he cana speaka

the italiano'. Bryan's assertion that he is 'part wog' is not, as he suggests, enough to gain him a pass in this subject.
GRADE: E

PHYSICAL EDUCATION
Mr K. Hall

Bryan's skills in most sports are fairly well developed, but he has no sense of 'team' whatsoever. He regularly berates, abuses, criticises, belittles and embarrasses his classmates for the slightest error, yet when he makes a mistake he always finds someone else to blame, including me on several occasions. His writing of his own name on the school's sporting equipment will also no longer be tolerated.
GRADE: E

WOODWORK
Mr D. Kenter

Bryan's relentless insistence on doing an impression of every tool as I mention them is, to say the least, very annoying. I'm well aware of what a drill sounds like, or a saw for that matter, and Bryan's time would be better served by taking this subject seriously. The coffee table that he submitted as his final assessment task still had the Kmart price tag on it.
GRADE: E

INTERPRETIVE DANCE
Ms K. Sharpe

Bryan's manipulation of his body shape allows for some weird and wonderful movement, contortion and convulsion. Without even trying, he has produced some amazing performances that have defied convention and even surprised himself. A career in interpretive dance beckons.
GRADE: A

was holding her left shoulder and grimacing. [If only Mick had seen that bump.] I then just lay on the ground holding my knee and within minutes we were both in the sick bay together. Strauchanie and Linda alone in a room with only a bed, a bottle of Dettol and a nurse who looked at least 113 years old – Strauchanie was genuinely frightened of her. It looked like her face had caught on fire and then somebody had tried to put it out with a bicycle chain. Truly frightening.

The craggy old school nurse kept looking at me and shaking her head, as she carefully put Linda's arm in a sling. She asked Linda if she'd like a glass of water, looked at me and shook her head one more time before leaving. Linda was just sitting there, staring at the floor, with a tear in her eye, her pretty face showing the strains of a first day not going to plan. Something inside told Strauchanie to break the silence. 'I'm sorry about bumping into you, knocking you into the rubbish bin and breaking your collarbone', I said.

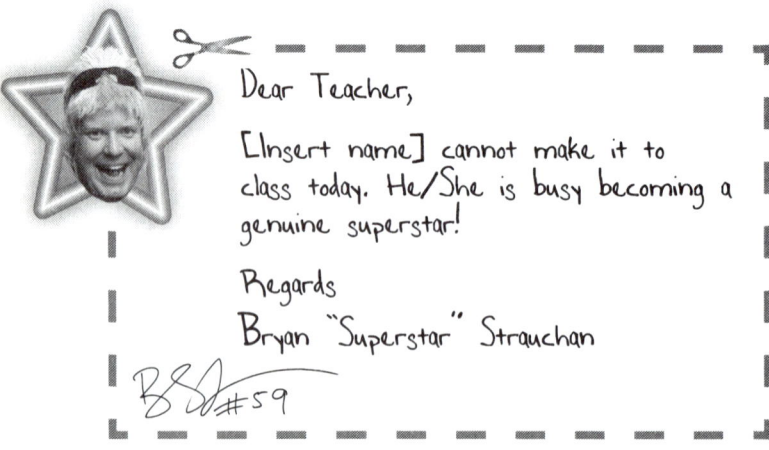

Dear Teacher,

[Insert name] cannot make it to class today. He/She is busy becoming a genuine superstar!

Regards
Bryan "Superstar" Strauchan

#59

Linda xxx

Linda slowly turned towards me. 'That's all right – you got me out of English', she chuckled. Strauchanie fell in love immediately and went in for the pash. 'My collarbone!' she screamed, as she jumped out of the way, so quickly that I did a face-plant into the window. The nurse came in, shook her head at me again and grabbed my leg really tightly. 'Show me your graze,' she bellowed, before pouring antiseptic on it. Strauchanie's scream could be heard all the way to the long-jump pit on the other side of the oval. She took pleasure in telling me that she'd run out of antiseptic and had no choice but to use vinegar instead. Linda couldn't help but giggle, and watching the last of her tears roll down her cheek and into her sparkling smile had Strauchanie all ga-ga. The nurse then pulled out the sick bay Polaroid camera to document our injuries. After she left, I picked up the camera and took a quick snapshot of Linda as she looked out the window.

Lucky I did because that was the last time I saw Linda. Her parents removed her from the school, as they feared for her safety. A more naturally beautiful girl Strauchanie is yet to meet. [Yes, I've met Chris Judd's girlfriend – she's OK. There's Christi – well, she's Christi, and Sarita Stella, cute but attached. Linda was in a different league. She was simply stunning.] I've carried that photo of Linda with me ever since. Sometimes I pull it out, look at it and wonder what ever happened to her. Part of me doesn't want to know and would prefer to leave the moment where it was. Which makes it even more disappointing that Craig Dyson rang me out of the blue recently to tell me that he and Linda had four kids and another on the way. It was a bitter pill for Strauchanie to swallow but having thought about it for a while, I realised that I will always have that moment in the sick bay with Linda Fratelli and the photo to remember it by … and I can kiss that photo whenever I want. Which, currently, is about four to five times a day.

There you go Matthew, Mark, Luke and John, that's how you write a chapter.

four

In the professional world of Australian Rules Football there are some things you simply cannot do without: boots; a mouthguard container; your club theme song as a ringtone; and, perhaps most of all, your teammates. If Strauchanie didn't have his teammates then he would look pretty silly taking on opposition teams on his lonesome. Although, he would give it a red-hot crack and could probably topple the Tigers. But the fact of the matter is that a football club is more fun with people in it, and you do develop a deep, unbreakable bond. I thought, there's no better way to introduce the parts of this inspirational book that are about my football career than by looking at the blokes who get to walk out onto the battle grounds of the AFL behind Strauchanie. It's a team game and Strauchanie cannot achieve individual success without teammates. Let's take an inside look.

1. LEON DAVIS – Loyal. Extremely loyal. Decided to stay at the Pies even when his brother Nick left for Sydney. Must be bloody tense at their Christmas parties.

2. SEAN RUSLING – Great body odour. Strauchanie often deliberately walks past him just to get a whiff. I think he is starting to get a bit suss about Strauchanie.

3. RYAN LONIE – Never actually met him.

4. ALAN DIDAK – Dittily, dittily, Didak. Didak Attack! Just when you thought the name Alan was being phased out, the hungry Croatian with the short legs brings it back with a whopping left foot from outside 50. Lost a little bit of respect for him when he smiled when Croatia scored against Australia in the World Cup. Strauchanie let rip 'Go back to where you came from Didak!' The next day Mick made me apologise to Dids and beg him not to go back to Port Adelaide.

5. NATHAN BUCKLEY – Buckanara! I think I say enough about Bucks in this book (see Chapter 6). We share something special: ultimate respect.

> Strauchanie has had a big impact on the culture of the playing group at Collingwood. He has bonded all of us. We once had a meeting that lasted four hours, just discussing ways we could trick him into training.
> **ALAN DIDAK**

6. BRODIE HOLLAND – McDreamy and Strauchanie have had their ups and downs. I was unhappy about him getting the gig on *Dancing with The Stars*, especially after the club had rejected Strauchanie's request to be on *Celebrity Overhaul*. Strauchanie has natural rhythm that cannot be taught, whereas Brodie dances like he is a garden hose that's been left unattended and turned on. Then, of course, he caught me in a compromising position with his model girlfriend Sarita Stella. I cannot stress this enough, but Strauchanie had just snapped off a loaf the size of a ~~Ford~~ Escort and the delightful Sarita was just helping me flush the damn thing down. Strauchanie and Brodie have a tense relationship.

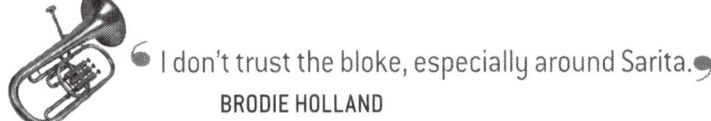

❝ I don't trust the bloke, especially around Sarita.❞
BRODIE HOLLAND

7. PAUL MEDHURST – Medibank thought he could just walk into the Lexus Centre and be a cult hero. Well, get in the queue because number 59 might be at the end of the line when it comes to the Guernseys, but when it comes to heroes, he is the first in line. As far as playing, Medibank is an opportunistic goal sneak with great hands and even better hair.

8. JAMES CLEMENT – Jimmy is Strauchanie's number one fan, but he is a complicated man, some may say strange. For one, I've caught Jimmy reading at times. I'm not talking about the *Footy Record* or the *Herald Sun* Footy Lift Out or the back of footy cards, Jimmy actually reads proper books. I threw out his copy of *The Catcher In The Rye* once because it unnerves me how much he reads. I replaced it with a copy of *Zoo Weekly*. Unfortunately, Travis Cloke found it and disappeared for forty minutes and put it back into the wrong locker. Ironically, I think it was Brad Dick's. In short, Jimmy is a champion of the club who I've been so proud to help develop with some subtle advice along the way. I know he appreciates it, I can tell by the way he doesn't speak to me. It's nerves. In awe of the Strauchanie aura. He is not the first and he won't be the last.

9. JACK ANTHONY – Poor fella suffered a neck injury which ruled him out of 2007. Personally, Strauchanie would have played with it. Strauchanie once won a semifinal for Horsham thirds after having a complete knee reco at half-time. Add to that a chest infection that even the club doctor described as 'nasty' and you have yet another amazing tale in the life of a superstar. My advice to JA was, 'Some people play through the pain barrier, Strauchanie jumps over the pain barrier!' He shook his head, probably thinking, 'What an inspiration.'

10. SCOTT PENDLEBURY – Former basketball champ who still refuses to play a little bit of one-on-one with Strauchanie. Don't blame him, Strauchanie has the aerial grace of Michael Jordan with the in-and-under know-how of Phil Smyth. He plays Dane Swan all the time, but we all know Dane Swan struggles to put the ball anywhere near the net. Pendles, if you're reading this, Strauchanie's comin' for ya!

11. SHANE O'BREE – The sad thing about Obi Wan is that he actually thinks he has Jedi mind power. I can tell that whenever I have an inspirational chat to him, he just stares blankly at me, as if he is trying to get Strauchanie to levitate in front of him. I said to him once, 'Obi, if you want Strauchanie to levitate, just pop the ball into the hot spot inside 50 and you will see a man leave the earth so high you will think you're at NASA.' Once I jumped so high in a preliminary final back at Horsham that the ump got so sick of waiting for Strauchanie to descend, he called play on. Didn't bother me, I snapped the goal, landed on the ground, gave out a couple of high fives and said, 'It's nice to be back boys, did you miss me?' They all shook their heads and thought, 'He will win nine Brownlows'. Embarrassed, I said, 'Let's save the compliments until after I've kicked 12' … unfortunately, due to the blustery conditions, I ended up kicking 1.9.

12. SHANNON COX – The Collingwood recruiting department needs to grow up. Don't get me wrong, there is nothing Strauchanie loves more than laughing at Adcock, Johncock and Dean Cox, but not within the walls of my own club. How can we be taken seriously with a Cox, a Dick and a Goldsack on the list? Can't wait for next year when Derek Hine and the recruiting staff draft Gary Boobs Jnr. Message: grow up!

13. DALE THOMAS – Tried taking the young fella under my wing and showing him a thing or two about life at the top, but he never listened. I took him aside during an ice bath after a game and said, 'If you want to be an elite footballer feel this ...' I grabbed his hand and went to put it on my quad, which I was flexing at the time. He took it the wrong way and jumped out of the bath and ran off. He was found three hours later in the weights room rocking in the foetal position. He missed five weeks but returned for the finals.

14. SHANE WAKELIN – Even Strauchanie is man enough to admit that Wakes is a good-looking man. Wakes, Lica and McDreamy Holland are probably the three blokes who come close to Strauchanie in the model stakes. I actually suggested to Wakes that the four of us, who I started referring to as 'Ocean's 4', should shower together without the other players. Wakes said he would take it up with the other boys. Never heard back.

15. CHRIS EGAN – Took my car park once and have never forgiven him.

16. NATHAN BROWN – He walked into the club and I said, 'Get back to the Tigers!' He quietly said, 'I'm not that Nathan Brown.' So, Strauchanie hit back with 'Go back to the Demons!' He replied, 'I'm not that Nathan Brown either.' Strauchanie said, 'Go back to Snoopy!' to which Nathan replied, 'That's Charlie Brown.' Bucks stepped in and suggested we get on with the Junior Footy clinic. Not sure what we can expect from Nathan Brown – they seem like they are a dime a dozen but there is only one Strauchanie.

There's no 'I' in Olympics or swimmer either, but Strauchanie likes to give support whenever needed.

Dunno why all car names get automatically crossed out when Strauchanie sends email from the ~~Lexus~~ ~~Centre~~. Annoying!

From: strauchanie@ ███████
Subject: SUPERSTR SUPPORT
Date: No thanks
To: thorpedo@ ███████

Dear Thorpedo,

G'day knackers, Strau-pedo here. Just thought I would drop you a B-Mail ('B' for Bryan!! lol) and say that you have Strauchanie's 100% support in your bid to clean your name from these outlandish claims of taking growth hormones. The whole thing is so bloody stupid, I mean, you can barely grow facial hair let alone be some abnormal apeman. I'll tell you what it is bro; it's the tall poppy syndrome. Think about it, all the greatest names in Australian sport they try to shame. Thorpe. Warne. Strauchan. Bradman. Phar Lap. The last one really irks Strauchanie, the poor fella was a horse who had no way of defending himself against the tabloid rumours of wild sex stable parties and that he faked his own death because his strapper, Tommy Woodcock, was getting too 'clingy'. To use your words Thorpedo, that is 'fully sick' [but not in a good way]. They went after Bradman next, saying he put too much milk in his tea and that it was a performance enhancer. Although Strauchanie has been told on good authority [by Williamstown coach Brad Gotch or 'Tamma-gotchi' lol!]

that ASIO has a secret file on Bradman saying he tested positive for Liptons and Rev after the Bodyline series. Makes you think, doesn't it? And poor Warnie, honestly, when will they just leave the bloke be? We're all champions, who cares if he wears Playboy undies, Strauchanie likes to freeball, what's it got to do with the price of tea in China?

I hope you clear your name, mate, because if there is one thing Strauchanie knows for sure, mud sticks. Strauchanie's name was dragged through the mud a while back, down at the Lexus Centre when a rumour got out that I was siphoning petrol from newbie Chris Dawes's car. Strauchanie protested his innocence vigorously. Tamma-gotchi then said that three players had seen me doing it [he didn't say who but I am guessing it was Travis Cloke, Sean Rusling and Ben Johnson]. I shouted, 'Strauchanie is innocent!' Guy McKenna then produced security tape footage of Strauchanie sucking on a hose coming out of Chris Dawes's ~~Daihatsu~~. I was furious at Bluey McKenna, making Strauchanie protest his innocence when they knew I was guilty all along. It was a lack of respect. I scratched Bluey's car on the way home that night, which he showed the playing group the next day on security tape. In fact, Bluey was sitting in the car when Strauchanie keyed his ~~Mazda~~. My point is: mud sticks. The playing group lost all respect for Guy McKenna for stitching up Strauchanie and he is still working hard to regain the players' trust.

Anyhow, Thorpie, chin up, I know you're in a hot spot at the moment but just remember you've been swimming through warm spots for most of your life so just keep swimming!

Strauchanie OUT!!!

17. SCOTT BURNS – 'Monty' Burns is a veteran of the club but still underrated in the AFL. Is it because he doesn't seek the attention? He doesn't crave the spotlight like McDreamy Holland, Bucks or Guy Richards, or is it because he has never been able to grow his hair long? His little mousy blond trademark has worked well for him, but if he wants to get noticed, try growing a rat tail at the back. He is originally from Adelaide, so it shouldn't be too much of an effort.

18. PAUL LICURIA – Lica is the heart of this club, after Strauchanie. He's always organising Spanish trivia nights. Last time, only Harry O'Brien and myself turned up. It broke my heart to see Lica reading questions at the lectern to an empty function room. Harry and myself sat on different tables to try and fill the room out a bit, but Lica knew the night was a shambles. He only got halfway through the first question, 'What was Ricky Martin's follow up single …?' before Strauchanie had taken the chance to jump to his feet and yell, 'She Bangs' but Lica had already left in tears. Luckily, Mick was working late that night and was able to console him. In the end, it turned out that I had told everybody the wrong night and that it was all my fault. I never told Lica, what would be the point? He was already feeling bad and I couldn't see the point in reversing that.

19. BEN DAVIES – Tries his best to look like Strauchanie but falls well short. Stole twenty bucks out of his wallet at training once and he never said anything about it. Nice kid.

THERE IS NO 'I' IN STRAUCHANIE

20. BEN REID – MS Readathon, as Strauchanie calls him, looks to have a big future if he lets Strauchanie teach him. He refuses to give Strauchanie his mobile number which makes it tricky for me to send him videos of me kicking goals on the boundary line. He has to keep in mind that, when Strauchanie's around, school's in.

21. GUY RICHARDS – Strauchanie calls him the Tall Guy because he is tall and he is also a guy. When I say he is tall, he is bloody tall. I took him to the movies once and he was booed during the entire screening of *The Hot Chick* which made it extremely tough for Strauchanie to follow the story-line.

22. RHYCE SHAW – Too quick for Strauchanie's liking. What's the point of handballing to somebody running past if they have already run past you? That's Strauchanie's secret, handball it to BS and I will always have time to pick it up on the way through. When Rhyce 'Yeah I'm' Shaw did his knee, I said to him as he grimaced in pain on the stretcher, 'This is the best thing for you, mate, it will slow you up a bit'. He took it well.

23. ANTHONY ROCCA – Pebbles is a BFG. A Big Friendly Giant. I like him because he laughs at all of Strauchanie's jokes. I once made Pepsi Max come out his nose and he hadn't drunk it for three days prior.

24. TARKYN LOCKYER – Despite trying to copy Scott Burns's haircut, Tarkyn 'Lock-It-In' is a good friendly bloke. He is second in the AFL in smiles, just behind Brad Johnson.

25. JOSH FRASER – Laid-back dude who gets on with the job. Cool, calm and collected. Strauchanie often says, 'Nothing frasers this guy'. I'm not just king of the nicknames but Strauchanie is also king of the one-liners!

26. BEN JOHNSON – I have been extra supportive of Johnno this year, as he goes through his man-vorce with Taz. It can be so hard, especially when there are fans involved. Johnno does a lot of charity work, a little bit too much for my liking. I told him to pull back on it a bit. 'You don't get Brownlow votes in the burns unit Johnno,' Strauchanie told him. He appreciated it, and I think you will find he reaps the rewards on the paddock.

27. NICK MAXWELL – Maxwell Smart has been controversially put into the leadership group ahead of Strauchanie. 'Why?' I imagine you asking. 'Was it racism? Put the Anglo in, instead of the Asian superstar?' I can't deny the same thought hasn't occurred to me. I see racism every now and then, and it stings. I recommended we watch *Crouching Tiger,*

Hidden Dragon before the Anzac Day game last year but no, Bucks suggested *Gallipoli*. He may as well have said, 'Get back in your rickshaw, Strauchanie, and go back to China!'

28. DANNY STANLEY – Mick described Stanley Knife as a bull of a player when he came down to the club. Lica once tried to invite him to one of his Spanish trivia nights – he'd thought of a sketch where he was dressed as a bullfighter taking on Stanley Knife pretending to be a bull, all to the tune of the Spanish language version of Shakira's 'Hips Don't Lie'. The Knife was not interested. Broke Lica's heart.

29. RYAN COOK – The Chef is a good bloke but, ironically, a disaster in the kitchen. He once made a toasted cheese sandwich for Strauchanie which had me running straight to the gents. Parked my arse into the cubicle next to Jimmy Clement, who was reading *Memoirs of a Geisha* to distract himself. I had to ask him to leave. Fair dinkum, Strauchanie was in bum rehab for a fortnight. The other blokes were laughing and giving The Chef high fives, but I have to ask the question: how do you bugger up a jaffle like that?

30. HARRY O'BRIEN – The Boy from Brazil or The Wax as I like to call him [or Windscreens, if I've just seen or heard the Windscreens O'Brien ad] has picked himself up from the poverty of Brazil in Africa and made something of himself. I am proud of him, especially because he came to Lica's Spanish trivia night.

Bryan, Brazil is not in Africa. Get your facts right or you could sound racist.

31. CHRIS DAWES – Every time I see Chris Dawes I start singing songs from the band, The Doors, which is funny, clever and entertaining. Everybody thinks it's hilarious. I made Strawberry Big M spurt out of Pebbles' nose when I sang 'Roadhouse Blues' as Chris walked into a team meeting. If you haven't picked it up yet, Strauchanie is the funniest bloke down at the club.

32. TRAVIS CLOKE – Trav was feeling pretty low after the club delisted his two brothers, Jason and Cameron. In fact, Strauchanie coined the phrase, 'Travis is now at Cloke Zero!' Strauchanie took the talented youngster aside and said, 'Blood is thicker than water, mate, and Collingwood is your family so forget everything else.' He started to well-up, it obviously meant a lot to him.

33. BRAD DICK – Obviously immature, although can't blame him entirely. What were his parents thinking?

34. ALAN TOOVEY – He giggles like a school kid every time I yell, 'Kick it Toovey, kick it Toovey'. I don't really even get it.

35. SIMON PRESTIGIACOMO – The man with the movie star good looks and the iron fist has actually been at the club for 32 years. Gets the job done whether it's stopping Matty Lloyd or baking a cake for Tyson Goldsack's surprise birthday party. Although, the cake for Sam Iles, shaped like a fit ball, was my favourite.

THERE IS NO 'I' IN STRAUCHANIE

MIXED TAPES

Here (at no extra cost) is Strauchanie's sure-fire list of songs to make a killer tape.

1. All Fired Up / PAT BENATAR (gets Strauchanie pumped up!)
2. Bound for Glory / ANGRY ANDERSON (probably written about Strauchanie)
3. Run to Paradise / CHOIRBOYS (Jenny!!!!!!)
4. Stutter Rap / MORRIS MINOR AND THE MAJORS (always gets a laugh ... shows Strauchanie's funny side lol)
5. The Final Countdown / EUROPE (Joey Tempest was the best front man since Jim Morrison)
6. The Living Years / MIKE AND THE MECHANICS (emotional)
7. Pants Around Your Feet song / NICKELBACK (this is funny and sexy ... classic)
8. Let Her Cry / HOOTIE AND THE BLOWFISH (Strauchanie nails this one)
9. Paradise City / GUNS N ROSES (Gunners!!!)
10. Summer of '69 / BRYAN ADAMS (HEHEHEHEHE!!!)
11. Get the Party Started / PINK (Strauchanie always does)
12. Up There Cazaly / MIKE BRADY (I like to change the words to 'Up There Strauchanie' — always goes well)
13. One Day in September / MIKE BRADY (not about 9/11)
14. Suddenly / ANGRY ANDERSON (chicks love this one!!)
15. Lips of an Angel / HINDER (serenade anyone??!!)

36. DANE SWAN – Every single time I see Dane I sing to him in a loud, booming, funny voice, 'Dane, you're not a Swan, you're a Magpie', and every single time he pretends not to laugh. I often feel sorry for people who aren't funny. Makes me sad, but then I sing 'Dane, you're not a Swan, you're a Magpie' and I am happy again and secretly, so is he.

37. SAM ILES – The Iles of Sam. I don't rate his haircut, looks like he is running around with a blond merkin on his noggin. However, Strauchanie is impressed with the way this fella moves on a dance floor. The second best duck-diver at the club, behind yours truly.

38. TYSON GOLDSACK – A man's lollybag is his own private man's business and Strauchanie does not approve of young Tyson making fun of it like that.

39. HEATH SHAW – Heath 'RU' Shaw has been a revelation because, to be honest, we all thought he was going to be a bit shit. Look at him now, he should be All Australian this year. Years ago, after training one night, I remember saying to Mick, 'Cut him, cut him now', to which Mick replied, 'You ran all this way to tell me that?' But Mick persevered and the rewards have been plenty.

40. CHRIS BRYAN – Big bloke from Carlton who I politely asked to change his surname because there is only room for one Bryan at Collingwood and his surname is Strauchan. He moon-slapped my forehead and walked away. Haven't spoken since.

THERE IS NO 'I' IN STRAUCHANIE

I put out the word that it would be polite if some of my team-mates could return the favour and talk about me for this chapter – this was left anonymously in my pigeon hole.

Strauchanie reckons it was B

Do NOT lend money to!

To whom it may concern

RE: MR BRYAN STRAUCHAN

Strauchanie has tried his best to be there for his teammates. He is the self-proclaimed morale booster around the club. Countless times we have limped off the MCG, some times in victory, some times in defeat, to find voice messages from Strauchanie on our mobiles. One message [obviously left at three-quarter time] had Strauchanie singing the Victory Blinds advertising jingle down the line. We lost that game by a goal. It was a tough message to sit through. Another he had left [at half-time, from the Cricketers Arms Hotel] had Strauchanie drunkenly singing Hinder's 'Lips of an Angel' before berating Bucks for handballing to Shane O'Bree instead of trying to kick a goal from seventy. He later explained that he was at the hotel because one of the coterie groups was having a function. We checked and there wasn't a function unless you include topless bar maids and seven blokes sitting by themselves a 'function'.

From some of the boys at the club,
who didn't want to be named

41. SHARROD WELLINGHAM – What kind of a name is Sharrod? Sounds like he is part of some weird cult. Have wisely kept my distance.

43. MARTIN CLARKE – A sad day when a bloke from Ireland gets a game for Collingwood ahead of Strauchanie. Honestly, what does he have that I haven't, besides a voice that's impossible to understand? I was at the canteen behind him once and I didn't know if he was ordering quiche or singing 'Sunday Bloody Sunday'. When he was finally finished, Strauchanie started singing 'Hooray Bloody Hooray'. Pebbles sneezed Fanta.

44. DANNY NICHOLLS – Danny Pickles offered me a handful of his cheese and chives chips once and, as a result, we will be lifelong friends.

45. BRENT MACAFFER – B-caf has posters of Matt Welsh and Lauren Newton in his locker. Strauchanie is too scared to ask why.

five 9!
Strauchanie lol!!!

The great Allan 'Yabby' Jeans once said, 'Players are like sausages. You can grill them, fry them or boil them, but they're still sausages.' No idea what it means, but boy am I hungry. Strauchanie better pop down to Bunnings and get a couple with onions to go. There's no doubt that Yabby is regarded as one of the greatest coaches of all time but really, that whole sausage analogy has more holes in it than a sausage that has had holes poked in it with a fork. Where Yabby falls down is that he's too general. You can't put all the players in the same sausage tray. They're different. Take Strauchanie, for instance. He's one of those gourmet sausages. Justin Koschitzke, on the other hand, is that sausage that keeps rolling around until it falls off the BBQ and lands on its head, and Brad Johnson is that sausage with a big smile on its face. [You can make a smile on a sausage using tomato sauce. Refer to Strauchanie's notes in the chapter: 'Dressing Up Sausages Like AFL Players'.]*

* Publisha-culpa: that (quite excellent) chapter edited out by meddling no-fun publishers before book printed.

STRAUCHANIE RATES HIS COACHES

Who knows, possibly 'Yabby' was on to something with the sausage thing. He did, after all, manage to win a few flags as a coach, the most memorable being St Kilda's one and only premiership in 1966. They beat the Pies by a point. Strauchanie would love to go back in time and change that result. I'd be just like Michael J. Fox in that movie *Back to the Future 3*. Although I doubt I could connect a flux capacitor to my ~~Ford~~ Cortina. Suffice to say, Strauchanie would only need to be on for a quarter and it's a ten-goal win. And if I wasn't tagged – a fifteen-goal win. Wow. Just think about it. Strauchanie going back to any time in football history. Imagine that: the 1970 grand final and just as Jezza runs towards Jerker Jenkins, Strauchanie sticks out his forearm and clotheslines him. Bang! Down goes Jezza like a Justin Koschitzke sausage. No more mark of the century. What about the '81 Grand Final? Strauchanie puts a close tag on Harmesy. When the ball's down the other end. Whack! Strauchanie throws a Horsham haymaker. No hitting the ball back to Kenny Sheldon for a dodgy goal. The only way Harmesy goes horizontal across the boundary line is on a stretcher. There's two ~~Toyota~~ commercials they'd have to re-shoot already! And who could forget the 2002 Granny. Anthony Rocca kicks what every Collingwood supporter at the ground thinks is the most important goal in the history of football. The goal umpire's just about to signal a point, when, in a moment of genius, Strauchanie starts celebrating with a combination Aka handstand, Mark Williams shotgun and Maori haka, leaving the goal umpire with no choice but to stick out the two fingers. It's a goal! They award Strauchanie two premiership medals for that one.

But let Strauchanie take you on another journey of sorts, one in which we look at the many and varied coaches that I have had throughout my career. There are those who have contributed to my success, have seen my potential and recognised my superstar qualities. There are those who I have made look good, and there was that one bloke who coached us in the Under 12s as part of his community-based order. Troy 'Stumpy' Peterson was his name. A short man, but a very scary-looking man. His head was shaved. Tattoos covered both arms. His elbows had spider-web tattoos. His earlobes had tattoos of stars on them and he had a tattoo of a bird on his neck. The end of his nose was all weird and spongy looking. Story has it that it was bitten off in a prison fight and the doctors had to rebuild it using skin grafts from his backside, which would explain why it had a couple of hairs growing out of it and why he kept scratching it.

Stumpy was destined to fall foul of the law. He came from a long line of troublemakers, thieves, petty criminals and all-round dodgy types. Three of his brothers were doing time for their part in a number of burglaries in the area, one of which was a job they did on the local footy club. It proved to be their downfall in the end. They incorrectly hooked up the stolen pie warmer when they got it home and their house burnt down. Members of the local fire brigade attending the fire were none too impressed to find some of their own possessions there as well, now charred and water damaged. [I think that's where Strauchanie's junior jumper went because it's disappeared. But in case it wasn't in the fire, I've got my spies keeping an eye out for it on eBay. If anyone out there has already purchased it and you paid less than $500 – you've got yourself a bargain!]

Despite his life going off the rails, Stumpy had a heart of gold. He'd pay us to pick stuff up for him, and then to deliver it. Pretty straightforward, and I was on more money than I got doing my paper round. To this day, I have no idea what was in the packages, but the guys in the tracksuits were always pleased to see me. Stumpy also taught us a lot. Like how to go in for the hard ball, how to gang tackle and how to fashion a knife out of a piece of tin and hide it down your sock.

We reached the grand final that year. The day started with Stumpy showing us an inspirational video. It was footage of him on *Crime Stoppers*. He'd knocked over a 7-Eleven. Unfortunately, in his haste he'd grabbed the wrong bags and ran off with four microwavable hot dog buns. There is, however, a lesson to be learnt from the video and that is: always stick to your game plan ... and when sawing off a shotgun, saw off the right end ... and never use your own car for the getaway, especially if it's got personalised number plates.

Dear Plaintiff,

[Insert name here] would like to settle out of court.

Regards
Bryan "Superstar" Strauchan

It must've fired us up 'coz we hit the ground running and by half-time we were up by 7 goals. The opposition couldn't touch us. In fact, they weren't going anywhere near us. My man was muttering something about them all having received threatening phone calls during the week. The police were saying the same thing when they arrested Stumpy ten minutes into the third quarter. He yelled at me to take over as he was being loaded into the divvy van. I wasted no time in implementing 'Strauchanie's Paddock'. Where 'Pagan's Paddock' gave Wayne Carey the forward line to himself, Strauchanie's Paddock gives me a bit more. Well, a fair bit more. Everyone else is confined to the back pocket. Didn't quite work as well as I'd expected, due mainly to the inability of my so-called teammates to follow team rules. Strauchanie handballs it to you, you give it straight back – it's pretty simple. We ended up getting rolled by 18 goals. Strauchanie must've left an impression on the opposition though. They chaired me off the ground. I was also quite

touched when they pulled me into their circle to sing the team song. As soon as that finished, I thought what the heck and led them in a rendition of 'We are the Champions'. By 4 am a group of us ended up egging my clubrooms.

Stumpy managed to arrange his day-release to coincide with our presentation night. He gave a stirring and emotional speech about the positive impact the time he spent with us had made on his life. He then made off with the bar takings and was never heard of again. Well, he thought it was the bar takings. In his haste, he grabbed the wrong bag and took off with the club's supply of urinal cakes.

At least Stumpy recognised Strauchanie's unique talents, which is more than I can say for my Under 14 coach, Gary Fowler. You see, Gary's son, Dylan, played in the team. Strauchanie was everything Dylan wanted to be, and so Dylan used his dad's position to advantage: everything Strauchanie wanted, Dylan got. You name it, the captaincy, the best and fairest, first in line on pie night, first in line for the leftover pies on pie night, first in line for the pies that some kids had only taken a bite out of. As you can imagine, Strauchanie was up against it. The real test of a person is how they handle a challenge. I said that once to Tarkyn Lockyer when he confronted me about parking in his spot at the Lexus Centre. He said that Strauchanie should know because I was more challenged in more areas than anybody he'd ever met. I thanked him for the compliment and told him that I wouldn't park in his spot tomorrow because I was planning on parking in Nick Maxwell's spot, or Max Nickwell, as I like to call him. [If you haven't noticed what

I've done, I'll explain it to you. I've swapped his first name which is 'Nick' with the first part of his surname, 'Max'. Nick doesn't like it but Strauchanie said, 'Hey, it's what I do. It's my thing. You can't stop genius. If you've got a problem with it, go and complain to Buck Nathanley.']

Under 14s was a very frustrating year for Strauchanie. Dylan was put on the ball every game, whereas Strauchanie was lucky to get on the ground at all. Dylan's Dad was doing everything possible to protect his son's grasp on the best and fairest trophy from the ever present threat of Strauchanie. He'd keep giving his reason for not playing me as 'team balance'. Don't talk to me about balance. I can drive a car while holding a zinger burger, chips and a Sunkist. It eventually got so bad that Strauchanie had no choice but to confront the coach. I told him, in no uncertain terms, that if I didn't start getting a fair go then I'd begin a public protest against his coaching methods. My campaign would begin with me boycotting the club canteen. Fortunately, there was a Coles Express nearby, so I didn't go without. The club canteen, on the other hand, dropped its revenue by more than half and found itself in dire financial straits. Gary Fowler was forced to reinstate Strauchanie to the team and to get his son Dylan to load up on canteen food to make up for the Strauchanie shortfall from the previous month. I then became the subject of a bidding war between the club canteen and Coles Express. The offers were quite comparable, but the club canteen was able to give me the cream on top. In fact, it was a whole barrel of cream. I bathed in it for four hours and I can tell you, my skin has never felt so replenished.

STRAUCHANIE RATES HIS COACHES

I didn't win the best and fairest that year. I'd left my run too late. The only consolation was that Dylan didn't win it either. He'd porked up so much on canteen food that he was unable to get out of bed for the last five games. Gary Fowler had to resign as coach and become Dylan's full-time carer. [The Collingwood dietician is always telling Strauchanie that what you put into your body affects how it performs. Presti's not an iceman in defence by accident. He has a Slurpee before each match. Dim sims are my energy source. Ten of them before a match and something inside my body says, 'Run, Strauchanie, run like you've never run before.']

I couldn't possibly discuss my coaches without spending some time talking about Mick. People say that his record speaks for itself. Sure, he coached West Coast to two premierships, but did the players really enjoy themselves?

Get over yourself Mick, and give Strauchanie a game!

```
From:     strauchanie@ ███████████
Subject:  STRAUCHANIE LIVING LEGEND OF LEGEND'S GAME
Date:     13 June 2007 9:58:23 PM
To:       mmalthouse@ ███████████
1 Attachment 63mb
```

Dear Mick,
   Did you see the Legends game? Was it embarrassing for you to see a man who you have not given a fair go for the Pies debut for the Big V? I would think so. Or are you going to be too proud and hide behind your little moustache and not care that you have the opportunity to help be a small part of the making of a genuine football superstar. I carved them up at the EJ, kicking goals from sixty, setting up goals, hard running, umpire abuse – Strauchanie gave it his all in front of 110,000 fans who just wanted a piece of BS. I have probably single-handedly revived Spud Frawley's coaching career. I told him at half time to instrument 'Strauchanie's Paddock' and he did, and all of a sudden it was raining goals! I hope you not giving Strauchanie a game has nothing to do with Strauchanie and Christi. We are both mature adult men with a knack for wisdom and a love of history [did you know the band Franz Ferdinand started World War 1? I can lend you a CD as soon as McDreamy Holland gives it back!] We need to put Strauchanie's and Christi's relationship behind us in the same way that Germany has moved on from their troubled past.
   All I will say, Mick, is watch the tape and in the words of ~~Mitshabischi~~ 'please consider'. Strauchanie has proven with his performance at the Legends game at the Dome and his BOG at the Shane Warne Foundation game at the 'G' that he is a big game player so if you are serious about winning a grand final anytime soon, then you '***must*** consider'.
   I have included the game as vid file, it may take a while to download. I have also included a video of a fat woman slipping over at her own wedding lol . . . omg hilarious.

Cheers
Strauchanie

Still waiting for response. Probably should haved cee-ceed Christi

I don't think so! He was far too disciplined. He's been out of there for a few years now and you only have to pick up the paper to see how much fun the Eagles players are having these days. Mick needs to lighten up a bit and it begins with his image. For starters, he can shave off that moustache and stop tinting his hair grey. Strauchanie's always wondered about Mick's moustache. Is it acting like a beard? What's he hiding? I was chatting to Tarkyn Lockyer at a club function and he was adamant that the mo was fake. I'd had a few Crown Lagers by this stage and was quite open to his suggestion that I was the man to give the mo a tug to see if it came off. A few other players had now joined the discussion and a kitty was building. It got to $7.50 and Strauchanie thought to himself, all right, let's do this. A few more Crownies for luck and I was away. I spied Mick across the room, chatting to a couple of supporters. I turned to the boys and gave them a wink and a thumbs up before breaking into a sneaky Strauchanie crawl, calling upon my ninja heritage. I arrived at Mick's shoes, looked up at the supporters, put my finger to my lips in a shushing motion and then, calmly, in the one slick move, stood up and reached around to Mick's face. As I felt the first bristle of moustache hair in the tips of my fingers, Mick's elbow rose in a split second, collecting me under the jaw and sending me up in the air and crashing down onto the life members' table. Mick's hiding something, all right!

I'll admit that Mick and Strauchanie's relationship has been a tad rocky. He certainly doesn't have me at hello and he doesn't complete me, but Strauchanie's ready and waiting for Mick to make his move. I guarantee, the day that he does and the day that Strauchanie and Mick align under the one common goal, then it will be a momentous occasion for the Collingwood Football Club. Unless Mick somehow stuffs his part up.

six

The history of football is littered with legendary partnerships. The Krakouer brothers, Nicky Winmar and Tony Lockett, Bobby Skilton and Adam Goodes, Daniel Ward and Simon Beasley. The list goes on longer than Strauchanie's little black book [not a racist book, just a book with chicks' phone numbers in it. At time of publishing Strauchanie had 97 numbers in it!!!]. The latest partnership though, possibly and probably the greatest of all time, is Nathan 'Bucks' Buckley and yours truly, Bryan 'Strauchanie' Strauchan.

At the end of 2004, a little fella waltzes down to Collingwood, armed only with a passion for the game and the promise that one day he will be captain of Australia's greatest sporting club. Of course the club already has a captain at the time, so Strauchanie would have to wait, wait in the wings, wait on the wing, wait on the flank, in the square, wait wherever he damn wants to because he is a genuine superstar. Observers are worried that there will be a clash of egos but they have nothing to worry about because Strauchanie has nothing but respect for Bucks, already a Brownlow medallist. So much respect, in fact, that Strauchanie is prepared to take Bucks under his ample wing.

Strauchanie took Bucks aside and whispered in the privacy of the Lexus Centre showers, 'I could show you a thing or two', with a wink and a smile. Unfortunately, this was taken the wrong way by the club legend and it took an alert Tarkyn Lockyer and Josh Fraser to break Strauchanie free from a vintage Nathan Buckley headlock.

After some calming down from Chris Egan, Bucks came over to apologise. Strauchanie appreciated this and promptly offered him a small handful of popcorn chicken. Strauchanie went on to suggest that Bucks should avoid using his left foot, that he shouldn't handball to Lica and if he ever gets to play alongside Strauchanie then he should always give off when the BS Express is steaming towards the 50. Bucks shook his head, grunted and walked back into the change room. No-one will ever know what the tired old champ was thinking, but I reckon Strauchanie could take a guess. He was thinking, 'Just when I thought I had nothing to learn, here comes this superstar in the making, straight out of the Horsham school of hard knocks, with hair like Brad Pitt, who has just dissected my game like a surgeon ... impressive, very, very impressive.'

The similarities in Bucks and Strauchanie are obvious. Both machines, with engines the size of Wangaratta. Both blessed with leadership skills recalling the likes of Winston Churchill, Nelson Mandela, Hulk Hogan and with a little bit of Ed Phillips thrown in. Seriously, Strauchanie was at a taping of *Temptation* once and there was almost a blue in the gift shop after one of the contestants disputed the sale price of a Bosch dishwasher. Strauchanie was about to step in and start throwing haymakers, Livinia was in tears and the models were hiding behind the dishes in their bikinis. [Between you and me Strauchanie copped an eyeful!!] Things were looking tenser than Mick Malthouse before Taz left, but then Ed Phillips stepped in. Boy did he step in! He spoke with the authority of a voice-over man, but with the grace of a male model showing off a windsurfer. Strauchanie hadn't seen anyone control a gift shop like that since Granny Mays in Horsham hired a Maori to handle store security. Let's just say, from then on, Strauchanie paid for his decks of nudie playing cards. Just like Ed Phillips led on that day in the *Temptation* gift shop, one day Strauchanie would lead the Pies.

Dear Bank Manager,

[Insert name here] cannot make this month's repayments because they upgraded their Foxtel package. Deal with it or I'll have to deal with you!

Regards
Bryan "Superstar" Strauchan

ME AND BUCKS

I told Bucks that story but I don't think he was listening. He was too busy texting Paul Licuria. Strauchanie couldn't help but think that was rude, so the next training session, during circle work, every time Bucks tried to drill me with a pass, I just stopped, got the old Nokia out and downloaded a ringtone. I think he got the message.

too obvious

A lot of the faithful down at Collingwood look upon Nathan Buckley as the perfect footballer, as if he descended from football heaven with a blind turn, shepherded by an angel. Well, Strauchanie's got news for all of them and I actually took the opportunity to tell them at the Copeland Trophy night after a few cheeky ones with Heath 'RU' Shaw and Rhyce 'Yeah I'm' Shaw. Just as James Clement got up to receive his second best and fairest medal, which, if I am not mistaken, is called the Wes Fellows Trophy, Strauchanie jumped up, half-cut. Jimmy didn't mind giving the microphone up, he respects Strauchanie and laps up any chance to hear the great man speak. It wasn't too long before Strauchanie had the crowd in the palm of his hand but, unbeknown to the fans, he was about to give the captain a slap. 'Good. Average. Footballer!' Strauchanie bellowed, pointing at Nathan. The Crown Palladium hadn't seen this kind of audacity since twenty minutes earlier when Strauchanie tried to take a specky over Ron Richards' granddaughter, which resulted in a bloodied nose. 'Hey, it's football, kid, accidents happen,' Strauchanie told the youngster as she was escorted from the venue by the St Johns Ambulance people. 'The problem with Bucks …' I continued, 'is he just doesn't put in. Sure, his hair looks

good, but a good head of hair doesn't win you grand finals. If it did, Strauchanie would have forty premierships by now ...' Strauchanie was obviously a bit tipsy at this stage, but I am man enough to admit that somebody probably spiked my Bacardi Breezer. If I was to point the finger, I would say Shane Wakelin. He was probably shirty at me because I kept calling him Mary-Kate and his twin brother, Ashley, after the Olsen twins from that classic old sitcom *Little House On The Prairie*.

'Doesn't give a hundred per cent,' Strauchanie screamed. 'Give me Ryan Houlihan any day of the week and twice on Sundays'. It was at this point that Strauchanie blacked out, possibly because he had gone too hard and too fast on the Breezers, trying to outdo Matty Lloyd's famous feat of five Bacardi Breezers on a Qantas flight from Melbourne to Dublin on the International Rules tour to Ireland. Whatever

(The publishers wanted this blacked out because Bucks would get too much correspondence.)

the reason, Strauchanie was somewhat happy to admit that he had gone too far, and I publicly apologised to Bucks in a private email I sent to his email address that he keeps strictly for mates and family: figjam@▓▓▓▓▓▓▓▓▓▓

Bucks appreciated the apology but I got the feeling he also appreciated the words I said on the night. Some blokes can't take criticism, David Fanning nearly broke down and cried once when he got me a Diet Coke instead of a Coke Zero at the canteen vending machine. Strauchanie let rip: 'You're as good at the vending machine as you are at doing circle work DF!' But Bucks was made of different stuff, tougher stuff, Made In Australia stuff, the kind of stuff they package mobile phone batteries in. Man, he was tough. Maybe Strauchanie's little outbust would be a turning point in the great man's career.

Let me be clear on this issue, Strauchanie has a great amount of respect for the man in the number five. The only criticism I have about him is that I don't think he takes football seriously enough. Take, for example, when Bucks took on the job as player representative on the Rules Committee. In the words of Fidel Castro, it was a 'disastro'. [Castro wasn't referring to Bucks, they haven't even heard of Bucks in Cuba. The only AFL players they have heard of are Jose Romero, Phil Narkle and you guessed it, STRAUCHANIE!!] So, Strauchanie gets on the phone to Bucks and suggests a few rule changes. They got totally ignored. Not long after, Bucks complains that no-one is listening to him on the committee. You don't have to be Johnny Holmes to work out the reason why – Bucks refuses to listen. I gave him about 12 suggested changes. The best being that whenever Hawthorn play the Kangas, instead of wasting everyone's time and boring everyone to death, just have first goal wins! Bucks pretended to type it into his mobile but I'm pretty sure he was texting Lica again. [Strauchanie thought about nominating as player representative when Bucks resigned from the Rules Committee but he probably won't have time due to the extensive author tour the publisher will be taking him on to promote this book.]

In the end, Strauchanie doesn't know what lies ahead for Bucks, I'm not a mind-reader. Although, I probably could read minds if I wanted, and Bucks probably reckons Strauchanie is the best kid he's seen walk onto an AFL paddock. It means a lot to Strauchanie to know that Bucks thinks that.

Bryan, we have only talked about a book signing in Horsham with your mother selling the books. This is not an 'extensive author tour'!

seven

Lachlan Quigley. Heard of him? Anybody? Didn't think so. He's not a household name. He should be though. If Strauchanie had his way, he would be. If Strauchanie had his way, fish and chip shops would develop a hybrid delicacy combining a dim sim and a potato cake, but Strauchanie doesn't always get his way. That's why I'm taking this opportunity to let everyone know about a 13-year-old boy called Lachlan Quigley. Not any ordinary 13-year-old boy, I might add. Not the kind of 13-year-old boy who would ride past your parked car, throw an egg at it and then yell, 'Lick it up ya fat *@*#!', before taking off, not quite fast enough to avoid being followed home and having his bike accidentally backed over a couple of times. No, Lachlan Quigley's not that sort of 13-year-old boy. Lachlan Quigley is a special boy. He mightn't go down in the history books like Burke and Wills did for discovering Tasmania, or Ned Kelly, or Swans player Paul Kelly, or Collingwood hard man Craig Kelly, or Dame Kelly Melba, or any other member of the Kelly Gang for that matter, but that's fine. He's still a hero to me. Let me take you back to when Strauchanie first met him.

Being born with amazing natural footballing ability is not something I take for granted. As an AFL player I have certain privileges and responsibilities. So, when I get an opportunity to give something back to the community, I'm more than happy to allow Strauchanie to involve himself in a bit of charity work and hospital visits, providing I'm not too busy making paid appearances. One day I happened to be walking into the Children's Special Care Hospital because I had parked across the road to buy a coffee scroll and didn't have enough coins for the parking meter. As I entered the lobby I stumbled upon an attractive, thirty-something, brunette woman, looking a bit distraught. Unable to assist me with my request for some spare change, she ran off crying into her hands. Concerned about her well-being, and still interested in her general hotness, I chased her down the hallway and into the lift. When the lift doors closed she turned around and, upon realising that I was in there, screamed, threw her handbag at me and said: 'Just take what you want, but please don't hurt me!' Twenty minutes later I'd managed to convince her, and hospital security staff, that all was above board [quite surprised none of them recognised me, actually] and I spent the next half-hour sitting with her as she told me the story of her son.

It was a heart-wrenching story. A story of pain. A story of struggle against the odds. But also a story of hope. Strauchanie could only listen and try to comfort her by holding her hand and rubbing that soft part of the inside of her leg, just above the knee. In circumstances like these, you think to yourself, there must be something I can do. 'Does your son, follow footy?' I asked.

'Yes, he absolutely lives for it,' she replied through her tears. 'He's Essendon through and through and has pictures of Matthew Lloyd all over his bedroom wall.'

I moved in a little closer and put my arm around her as I prepared to tell her something that would change their lives forever. 'So, he loves his footy, does he? Maybe I can help?'

Her eyes popped wide open and sparkled in anticipation. 'Do you know Matthew Lloyd?'

'No, well, I have met him, but it's not often that you can get two superstars in the one room at the same time. It's not like we have a Superstars Club and we all gather on a regular basis.' [Although Strauchanie must admit he did think the idea has merit.]

You could feel the air shoot out of her lungs as she sighed. 'Oh, well, never mind.'

'There is something I can do,' I said. 'I can pay your son a visit.'

❝ The year I had out of footy was the most frustrating in my career and seeing Strauchanie struggle with chronic chafing has reminded me how lucky I am to be back fit and playing our great game. ❞

MATTHEW LLOYD, Essendon captain

Her response was not as enthusiastic as I expected. 'That's OK, thanks anyway but, as I said, he's Essendon mad and …'

But I was insistent. 'Leave it to me. Strauchanie has universal appeal. Everyone would love him to be at their club [not that Mick realises it]. Just tell me what room he's in and I'll surprise him.'

Hospitals have a certain smell about them. Just as football change rooms do, and just as a two-week-old souvlaki that has been sitting on the floor of your car does. But it's the smell of hospitals that makes me feel really uneasy. This can be attributed to the many operations I've had over the years, beginning with my appendix being removed when I was ten years old. Something I'll never forget, especially the moment when I awoke from the anaesthetic. I pulled the appendix out of a jar next to my bed and took a bite out of it, thinking it was a pickled gherkin. But who am I to complain? Young Lachlan Quigley has been in and out of hospitals his entire childhood life.

As I approached Lachlan's room, a number of thoughts began rushing through my head. Firstly, how lucky am I? Not only being in perfect health, but also in peak physical condition. Secondly, why are only some of us chosen to achieve greatness? And thirdly, I wonder if this children's hospital has a McDonalds?

Before I knew it, I was standing outside Lachlan's room. Room number 59. How weird's that? Strauchanie's jumper number – 59. A friendship that was meant to be. This called for a grand entrance. I took a deep breath and then, in

BRYAN STRAUCHAN: MY STORY

> As well as sick kids, Strauchanie also likes to help handy-looking chicks in trouble, and since my own brush with the law (see page 88) I felt I could really reach Schapelle (and maybe get an in with her sister).

From: strauchanie@ ▇▇▇▇▇▇▇▇▇▇
Subject: ~~MERCEDES~~
Date: yes please!
To: Corbs@ ▇▇▇▇▇▇▇▇▇▇

Dear Schapelle,

How's it hanging Corbs? Strauchanie here. Just thought I would drop you a line to let you know we are all thinking about you back here in Australia. I have taken time out of my busy training schedule (have trained three times in the last fortnight) to inspire you to survive the hellish conditions of that Balinese jail you are shacked up in. I know how you feel, sometimes the Lexus Centre can feel a bit like a prison but instead of bars, there are electric sliding doors; instead of prison wardens, there are conditioning coaches; and instead of machine guns, there are witches hats and whistles. Some of my cellmates are probably just as nasty too. Nick Maxwell cut one during recovery the other day that even made the team mascot's eyes water and he's made out of cotton and stuffing. Newbie Ben Reid is always hassling me for a lift home just because we live next door to each other. Last Wednesday after training, Strauchanie had to hide in the hydraulic chamber for nearly three hours before MS Readathon finally got the bus home. Sure, my hamstrings are feeling better than ever but I missed the first half of *House*. Strauchanie not happy. Shower time here can be pretty full on at

STRAUCHANIE
COLLECTABLES

Apart from the bonus of getting Strauchanie in colour, these are extra bonuses as this footy card will be worth a heap one day.

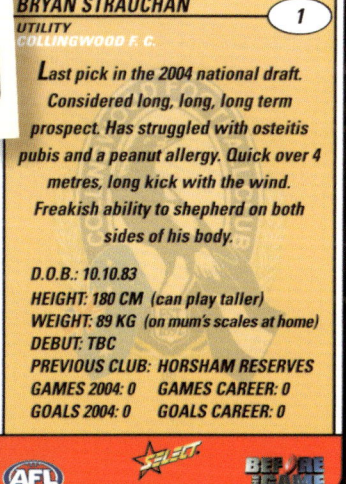

Bryan, see the query on page 22. According to your story you are 18 or 19 but now it looks like you're 24!

Again - see pages 20-21 for explanation - BS

STRAUCHANIE AND FRIENDS

One of the greatest partnerships of all time … Nathan 'Bucks' Buckley and yours truly, Bryan 'Superstar' Strauchan.

'There will never be another Strauchanie and the boys at the club can only be grateful for that.' (Bucks)

STRAUCHANIE SUPERSKILLS

TOP LEFT: Strauchanie's early ability in interpretive dance is evident here

TOP RIGHT: Strauchanie's trademark style

LEFT: The kicking action that got Strauchanie a goal in the Legends game

STRAUCHANIE IS A LEGEND!

Strauchanie's debut game, 13 June 2007, E.J. Whitten Legends game, known forever more as 'The Strauchanie Show'.

Why dance in your bedroom when you can dance at the ball?

the Lexus Centre, you do not want to drop the soap here trust me . . . because if you do it's twenty push ups and a ten dollar fine. I saw your sister on the news the other night, I can't print her name because it compromises my relationship with one of our major sponsors and all letters and emails are checked before being sent from the Lexus Centre. Jimmy Clement once sent a letter to a mate recommending he watch films by famed director Francis ~~Ford~~ Coppola and he was suspended for two weeks. Ben Johnson wrote a fan letter to Mark ~~Holden~~ and got a week. Scott Pendlebury was seen eating an Iced Vovo but mistakenly called it an Iced ~~Volvo~~ and was almost traded to Richmond as a result. We all live in fear, as I am sure you do. Have you considered a karaoke night to help lift your spirits? Strauchanie is the king of karaoke. The key is being able to rock it out with a song like 'Living On A Prayer' but then bringing it back with 'Everybody Hurts'. The last time I sang 'Everybody Hurts' before the Freo game there was not a dry eye in the house . . . it was only later that Lica informed me that Maxwell had cut another one.

Anyway, I should push off as this ice bath is starting to cause some serious shrinkage and young Nathan Brown (not the Tiger or Demon, another Magpie newbie) is getting sick of taking dictation. I have included a Strauchanie poster in case you want to break out of prison 'Shawshank' style.

Love always
Strauchanie ☺

PS: Are you really sharing an email with David Hasselhoff or was that a joke email that Shane O'Bree sent me?

PSS: Was Paris in your prison?

PSSS: Say hi to ~~Mercedes~~ for me.

typical Strauchanie fashion, I jumped around the corner and into the room with my hands in the air yelling, 'Strauchanie!' I was in the wrong room. There was an old bloke in there getting a catheter removed. I quickly pulled out a texta, signed it and left.

Turns out Lachlan was in room 49. I should've been paying more attention to what his mum, in the tight skirt and revealing top, was saying earlier. Couldn't really remember what illness he was suffering from either but, by all accounts, it was a pretty nasty one.

I finally arrived at Lachlan's room. A skinny, oldish, grey-haired nurse was just leaving. She put her finger to her mouth and whispered that he was asleep. I put my foot in the door as she tried to close it. I explained who I was, but I could tell from the expression on her already wrinkly face that she wasn't going to let me in. A minor scuffle developed. We both got in a few jumper punches before I was left with no choice but to put her in a Brendan Fevola-style headlock. She managed to release herself by biting me on the tummy. She then grabbed my arm, twisted it behind my back and forced me against the wall. A crowd began to gather. Then, just as I was about to unleash some patented Strauchanie judo moves, a couple of interns pulled Strauchanie off her. While they were holding me back she got in a couple of cheap shots and then disappeared. Come to think of it, one of the interns may have thrown a couple of sneakies as well. Feeling a bit sore and sorry, I comforted myself with the knowledge that I would be storing that incident in my memory for when the opportunity arrived for some payback.

[The memory bank is getting pretty full, so Strauchanie may have to lose the one about the guy at the bakery who sold me a cream bun with significantly less cream on it than usual.]

The sleeping Lachlan looked so calm and peaceful. With his dark hair and olive complexion, he looked like a young, weedier version of Paul Licuria. Lachlan should be happy with that. The ladies think that Lica's a bit of all right. Not that I'd know. I wouldn't know which players were good looking or what order of good lookingness they'd be in. Although, if you were below Heath Shaw on the list, you'd be worried.

I got to thinking, if Lachlan knew that Strauchanie had been there and he'd slept through it, then he'd understandably be a very disappointed young man. So, what better way to wake him up than break into a gut-busting rendition of 'Good Old Collingwood Forever'? The Strauchanie version, that is. I simply replace 'Collingwood' with 'Strauchanie'. Shane O'Bree loves that version. He gets me to sing it to the players all the time. They piss themselves. Shane can't get enough of it. He got me to record it for him as his ringtone.

So, anyway, I counted myself in ... a one, a two, a one, two, three, four ... five, six, seven ... *Good Old Strauchanie forever* ... and bang! Lachlan sits bolt upright, looking like you do when you've had an afternoon nap, your alarm goes off and you've got no idea what day or time it is. I immediately called, 'heads up,' as I handballed a football in his general direction. With his hand–eye co-ordination not at its best, owing to him being heavily sedated, the ball smacked Lachlan fair and square in the face. A few seconds passed before a wide robotic smile appeared. He fell back onto his pillow and slowly drifted off into a deep sleep again. I thought, well, I've done all I can for today. I left my number with his mum, so that we could arrange the next visit. I asked for hers, but she couldn't find her phone and was having a mental blank about her number. I told her that it wasn't a problem and that I would pop in to see Lachlan next week. I could pick her up if she liked. Even make a day of it. Start with a bit of lunch, visit Lachlan, maybe catch a movie and then who knows where the night will take us from there. Unfortunately, before we could organise anything, she had to rush off because she was worried she'd left the iron on.

I said my goodbye to the sleeping Lachlan, kissed him on the forehead and left. As I was walking down the corridor, who did I see coming towards Strauchanie? None other than Essendon champion Matthew Lloyd. I greeted Lloydy with a handshake. There's a special bond between AFL footballers. Unless you've experienced the intensity, the pressure and the demands of a professional sport at an elite level, then you wouldn't understand. It's something people who have been to war can relate to, and similar to the experience of those who, along with Strauchanie, queued up for days waiting for the first Krispy Kreme doughnut franchise to open in Australia.

'What are you doing here, Lloydy?' I asked.

'I'd heard about Lachlan's plight,' he replied, 'and was coming to personally deliver a signed Bombers jumper.'

FYI: Number of books by Lloydy = 0

THAT SPECIAL BOY

I was immediately on the defensive. 'I've got Lachlan covered thanks, Lloydy. Go find your own kid. It's a big hospital, full of sick kiddies and you're trying to move in on mine.'

Lloydy was a bit affronted. 'But Lachlan's an Essendon supporter. I'm sure he'd be happy to receive this.'

'All right, all right, Lloydy, leave the jumper with me and I'll pass it on. There's no point seeing Lachlan anyway – he's asleep.'

Lloydy stuck his head in the door, saw for himself that Lachlan was asleep and then handed over the jumper. 'Don't forget to give it to him.'

With a wry grin on his face, Lloydy shook his head at me and then left. It was as if we were in a game and I'd kept him goalless and he'd been dragged.

I couldn't believe the nerve of Lloydy, trying to trump me like that by offering Lachlan a signed Essendon jumper. Fortunately, I was able to off-load the Lloydy jumper on eBay while, at the same time, picking up a Nutri-Grain that looked like Sean Rusling and still have twenty three-bucks left over.

I eventually did get back to see Lachlan. It was a couple of weeks later and I'd decided to give him a pair of Strauchanie's footy boots from last year's Round 2 victory in which I probably would've kicked five, had I been playing. As I approached Lachlan's room something didn't feel quite right. I hesitantly walked in, only to find that his bed was empty and freshly made. I grabbed a passing nurse and asked where Lachlan was. She put a supportive hand on my shoulder and said, 'I'm afraid he's gone.'

I felt numb. My heart sank as I slowly sat down on the chair and put my boots on the bed. 'Gone?'

'Yeah, to Queensland. The whole family moved up there for his dad's work.'

Tears welled in Strauchanie's eyes, 'Is he going to be all right?'

'I think so. Tonsillitis usually takes about two weeks to recover from.'

Strauchanie slept well that night and lucky he did, for little did he know that soon he would have his own battles to face.

eight

Who are the most famous adoptees you can think of? Maddox Jolie, Davey Madonna, Gary Coleman, Todd Bridges and the kid in Grade 4 who always had a runny nose. Before Angelina Jolie started racking up the kids on the old adoption expense account, there was one other pretty famous adoption story that has only recently come to light. So, add this one to the list ... Bryan 'Superstar' Strauchan.

Hard to believe, isn't it? How could someone give Strauchanie away? Imagine winning the lottery and being the solo winner of six to eight billion dollars and throwing the ticket away. You would feel pretty bloody silly, wouldn't you? I haven't bothered to track down the bozo's who gave me away, but, I have to say, I am so glad they did. Because, despite not gestating in my mother's womb [that's Soy Bean] and despite not entering the world through her 'lady cavity', I still consider myself an Australasian.

I won't lie: finding out that Soy Bean was not my natural mother was tough. I found myself questioning everything in my life: my heritage, my identity, my place in the world, my diet ... the only thing Strauchanie never lost faith in was his ability to snag goals from the boundary on his left, while running at full speed. I became estranged from Mum for a while, I couldn't look her in the eye, I couldn't stand to hear her voice and even her shark fin soup suddenly had a bitter taste. Strauchanie was at the crossroads like Britney Spears in that movie *Beaches*. It was time for Strauchanie to dig deep, just like in the semifinal for the Horsham thirds when we were down by three points at three-quarter time and Strauchanie was told by the club doctor that they may have to amputate Strauchanie's right leg. Strauchanie, showing true grit, kicked the Doc in the nuts with his left and said to the coach, 'Put me in the middle!' Everyone thought I was crazy but when Strauchanie speaks, people tend to listen.

Thirty-three minutes later, Strauchanie was in the dressing rooms having a beer. Unfortunately, we lost the game by nine goals. We were smashed in the centre clearances. The good news was I kept my leg, with the doctor explaining to me that it was actually just a bit of cramp. The football gods have a funny way of smiling down on you. It was actually the last final Strauchanie played in, after missing the following twelve months of footy with chronic chafing. It is bloody hard to get over chronic chafing because you can't train with it. Fair dinkum, during one session of circle work, Strauchanie nearly started a fire between his thighs and no, ladies, not in a sexy way. My comeback was against-the-odds stuff – the word around Horsham was that Strauchanie was finished but they didn't

BRYAN STRAUCHAN: MY STORY

> Included to show I've always had a thing about capsicum spray. In books we call that a 'recurring theme'.
>
> FYI: Number of recurring themes in Hirdy's book = 0

POLICE INCIDENT REPORT

REPORT No: 2573348
DATE: 29th June 2006
TIME: 4am
LOCATION: Flinders Lane, Melbourne

OFFENCE: Public Urination
REPORTING OFFICER: Constable Steven Hunter

SUSPECT DETAILS:
NAME: Bryan Keith Strauchan
AGE: 21
ADDRESS: Not given

DETAILS OF OFFENCE: Driving down Flinders Lane, Constable Bennett and myself noticed a commotion. The gathered crowd quickly dispersed revealing a male suspect, pants around his ankles, urinating on a shop front with both hands in the air, yelling 'Strauchanie!' Upon approaching the suspect he threatened us with the words, 'Don't come any closer, this thing has a range of 15 metres.' When we asked the suspect for his name he responded with, 'Give me two minutes and I'll spell it out for you.' Which he did, by pointing himself towards the middle of the road. With a few swivels of his hips, he'd written the word 'Strauchanie', even managing to dot the 'i'. His refusal to co-operate left us with no choice but to tackle him to the ground. Once handcuffed the suspect was placed in the back of the police car and taken to the station to sober up. For the entire journey he made the 'you should use that capsicum spray on your pizzas' joke no less than ten times.

count on the one thing that cannot be measured: the size of Strauchanie's heart. The following year I was back playing, although I missed thirteen weeks for misconduct after I got a hold of some capsicum spray from a teammate's locker [he was a copper in his spare time] and Strauchanie let rip into the ump's eyes in the car park after the game. Luckily for the ump, he was wearing glasses. He was probably on the way to the library, but Strauchanie let him know what he thought of his efforts on the day. 'If you're gonna umpire like you're blind, then you may as well be blind, albeit temporarily!'

Strauchanie represented himself at the Wimmera Tribunal and some legal experts have since said that it was the best defence in a courtroom since Jack Nicholson in *A Few Good Men*. The local paper was calling for the umpire to serve time after I was finished with him. Truth be told, I actually ripped the speech off from Jack Nicholson verbatim and you should have heard the chills in the courtroom when I screamed at umpire Hoxley, 'You can't handle the truth!' In hindsight I probably should have changed some more of the names and references, but I was on a roll. Below is the official transcript as provided by the Wimmera Football League Tribunal.

Strauchanie: You want answers?

Hoxley: I would like to know why you tried to blind me with capsicum spray?

Strauchanie: You want answers?

Hoxley: It's just a game of football, it should never . . .

Strauchanie: You can't handle the truth! Ump, we live in a world that has walls. And those walls have to be guarded by men with guns. Who's gonna do it? You? You, umpire Hoxley? Strauchanie has a greater responsibility than you can possibly fathom. You weep because your eyes got peppered, and you curse the Horsham Football Club. You have that luxury. You have the luxury of not knowing what Strauchanie knows: that Santiago's death, while tragic, probably saved lives. And Strauchanie's existence, while grotesque and incomprehensible to you, saves lives … You don't want the truth. Because deep down, in places you don't talk about at parties, you want Strauchanie on that wall. You need Strauchanie on that wall.

[margin note: should have changed this bit]

We use words like honour, code, loyalty … we use these words as the backbone to a life spent defending something. You use 'em as a punch line. Strauchanie has neither the time nor the inclination to explain himself to a man who rises and sleeps under the blanket of the very freedom Strauchanie provides, then questions the manner in which Strauchanie provides it! I'd rather you just said thank you, Strauchanie, and went on your way. Otherwise, I suggest you pick up a weapon and stand at post. Either way, Strauchanie don't give a damn what you think you're entitled to!

Hoxley: I am recommending you receive 16 weeks.

Strauchanie: *(quietly)* I did the job you sent me to do.

BEFORE ANGELINA...

Hoxley: Who are you talking to? Make it 18 weeks.

Strauchanie: You're goddamn right Strauchanie did!!

There was not a dry eye in the tribunal. The committee decided to give me a reduced sentence of thirteen weeks. They also recommended that I go on to teach drama at the local high school, where they were about to begin rehearsals for the stage version of *Footloose*. I had to resign in the end because, when I let rip with the 'everybody cut, everybody cut…' bit, my chafing would flare up again and no amount of wearing bicycle shorts and cornflour seemed to help.

You may be thinking, what has all this got to do with adoption? Well, as a matter of course, Strauchanie overcomes obstacles. Strauchanie leaps over hurdles [not literally, the chafing again!]. My people built the Great Wall of China, the biggest obstacle of them all. MEGA Obstacles are in my blood. Strauchanie went for his driver's licence in a car that had a dodgy clutch and a dead body in the boot. I avoided

OK, fixed - BS

I think you mean "metaphorical" obstacles here.

> When Strauchanie was lost, he came to me. I helped him get back on track … obviously not the training track but the path of life. Ever since, he has sent me deep fried fortune cookies, some of them have a little note of wisdom but most just have parking fines he hopes I can waive.
>
> The Right Honourable JOHN SO, Lord Mayor of Melbourne

Bryan, please provide evidence that Mr So said this, or delete! Yes, he has the power to waive my fines - BS

cops, trees and roadblocks and still came in with a perfect score of 83.

My career this year was railroaded when the chafing came back. Honestly, it was like there was a fire in my shorts every time I tried a lunge. But just like the greatest Chinese warriors [even the ones made from terracotta] Strauchanie fought on and got the best out of himself.

When Strauchanie found out he was adopted I could have dropped my bundle and driven myself headfirst into a buffet [I only did that twice] but Strauchanie got motivated instead. Like I said earlier, Strauchanie doesn't care if he popped out of a Chinese vagootz or an Aussie vagootz, my mum's my mum, family is family and that's just the way it is ... until they start asking for finals tickets, and then I screen my calls like the FBI. I don't mind being the poster boy for adoption, and if it helps adoption awareness maybe Angelina could adopt Strauchanie as well. And if that happens I may just have to get back on the boob ... Strauchanie!!

Possible shot for poster boy for adoption campaign

OK, Bryan, perhaps this explains some of the confusion about your early family history.

nine

> After the Eddie boning for ignoring Strauchani's tv show ideas, I expect new ch 9 head to be pretty keen to chat soon — but forget it copy cats, Strauchanie has outwitted you and copyrighted them all (by putting this © here).
>
> FYI: parts of Hirdy's book worth copyrighting = 0%

When you have two high profile, respected and powerful media identities at the one club, there are always going to be clashes. In the case of Edward Joseph McGuire and Bryan Keith Strauchan, it is hotter than cooking dim sims in a sauna, which, incidentally, is now banned after Strauchanie tried to steam a few cheeky ones at a recovery session. Don't get me wrong, Strauchanie has a decent amount of respect for Eddie and he has made some pretty impressive decisions down at Collingwood, but there are some that have completely baffled Strauchanie and Strauchanie don't baffle easily. In fact, the last time I was truly baffled was when Smorgy's introduced a vegetarian section in their Wednesday buffet, honestly if you're a vego, what are you doing at Smorgy's?

First of all, Eddie set up the Lexus Centre. Good move. Seriously, Strauchanie can't help but laugh when he visits other clubs and sees how they live. I went down to meet Rodney Eade in what I thought was an abandoned warehouse and 'Blast Off' told me that's where they train. I nearly choked on my cornflakes. I was actually surprised they even had cornflakes to offer me. Then, of course, there are the poor old Kangaroos at Arden Street. It was a crap heap before it burnt down. In fact, I think the fire caused $25 000 worth of improvements! Actually, Strauchanie can't claim that zinger, I heard one of those comedians on that *Before The Game* show do it, in fact, I think they all did that gag at one time or another. By the way, I can't believe they didn't catch the guys that did that. The fire was started with two car tyres. Now, you don't need to be CSI Horsham to work out that there's a car driving around North Melbourne with two of its tyres missing. Anyway, why pick Arden Street to burn down? Was there any need to get Glenn Archer angrier than he already is?

Strauchanie was immediately concerned that the same thing could happen at the Lexus Centre, so I suggested we start our own fire brigade. We could all take shifts. It would be good for team bonding, morale and an excuse to break into Scott Burns' locker and read his poetry. I suggested that I take on the first night watch with Ben Johnson, Scott Pendlebury and Ryan Lonie. All left-footers, come on, think again Strauchanie! Pretty predictable as to which side they'd favour when fighting a fire. Fires would pick up on their preferred side and just change tack. I also decided against joining the watch because I'd always suspected it was Scott Pendlebury who threw a hot chilli down Strauchanie's bum crack during a preseason jog. I bent down to do the old shoelaces up and all of a sudden in the words of Lou Richards 'it was on for young and old'. [This was spooky. Remember how my grandmother died in a shoelace accident? Was it a genetic thing?] The chilli had landed and I made the near-fatal mistake of clenching instead of pouting. Before you know it, Strauchanie had parked his bot bot into the iconic Yarra River. Not a pleasant experience, with Strauchanie's arse acting like one of those rubbish collector traps. I reckon I pulled out three empty chip packets, two beer cans and a shopping trolley, all wedged up my clacker.

I went straight to see Eddie about it. This kind of insubordination would not be tolerated at the club, at least not when it involved putting spicy foods down Strauchanie's date. Eddie laughed in disbelief. He slammed his hand on the table, still laughing in disbelief. He wiped tears away

---

PAGE 96:

You refer to your grandmother's death and your concern that you could be genetically predisposed to suffer the same fate. Ignoring the unlikelihood of a genetic phenomenon of "death by shoelace", Bryan you are adopted, so do not share any genetics with your grandmother.

Yeah, but leave in as now have twice as many recurring themes than Hirdy does in his book – BS

from his eyes, tears of disbelief, I was sure. He told me, 'These things happen at a footy club, Strauchanie, it's part and parcel. It's character building. Now, if you don't mind, I'm reshuffling the Monday night programming on Nine.' He then reminded me that, technically, Channel 9 was still out-rating Channel 7. He went to grab a print-out of the demographics and all the people statistics to support his claims before I stepped in. 'I just think something needs to be done. It's about respect. I'm a future Brownlow medallist. Can you imagine Scott Pendlebury putting a chilli down Bob Skilton's clacker? Soon they'll all be ganging up on Strauchanie. It'll be like one versus one hundred, they're like a bloody mob'. Eddie looked at me the way he looks at Bucks, with passion and purpose. 'Strauchanie, you're a genius!' I left as Eddie started writing on his pad furiously. He seemed happy and that made me happy. I was sure there would be no more problems.

97 the number of chicks in Strauchanie's little black book! (see page 66)

When I returned to the rec room, the boys were playing cards. Texas hold 'em poker. I'd never played before but they promised to help me along the way. Very confusing rules. When Benny Johnson got three-of-a-kind, it beat my two pair, but when I got three-of-a-kind, it didn't beat his two pair, because I was on the left-hand side of the dealer. Being on the left-hand side of the dealer cost me a few hands that night. I'll make sure I don't sit there again. The poker game was brought to a screeching halt when the phone rang. I jokingly said, 'Maybe it's Cameron Ring?' The boys didn't laugh ... must have gone straight over their heads. So, I said it again. 'Maybe it's Cameron Ring from Geelong?'

BRYAN STRAUCHAN: MY STORY

Still nothing. So, I went again. 'Maybe it's Cameron …? Benny Johnson cuts me off: 'Yes, we get it, Strauchanie!'

It wasn't until later that night, when Strauchanie was watching *Joker Poker*, that I realised I had been the victim of a scam. The boys had stitched me up. I had lost nearly three hundred dollars. Livid, I marched into Eddie's office. He was on the phone to one of the Nine head honchos. It was on speaker phone and they were yelling 'mob, mob, mob!'. I thought it was weird, but I couldn't be arsed thinking any more about it. I told him what had happened. Eddie's disbelief was twice what it was the day before. The laughing, the slamming and the tears were followed by a dash to the bathroom. Strauchanie waited for a while but Eddie didn't return, so I stole a few business cards and left.

Bryan, see opposite. I find it hard to believe that Mr Bracks said this. Please show me (in writing). Otherwise delete.

STRAUCHANIE v EDDIE

Later, when I realised that I may have unwittingly given Eddie an idea for a Channel 9 game show, I started making calls to his office and then his mobile and then his home phone suggesting ideas for other TV shows. One of my favourites was a sitcom about a Collingwood veteran moving into a one-bedroom apartment called *The Burns Unit*. Another one was a prank-style show called *Leon's About*, where Leon Davis plays tricks on unsuspecting commuters. If Leon wasn't up for it, Strauchanie also pitched *Egan You On*, the same idea but with Chris Egan. Then there was *Thank God You're Harry*, where Harry O'Brien walks through a door and has to deal with different situations that are thrown to him. A magic show called *Hey Presti* featuring Simon Prestigiacomo. *Swanning About* was another one, featuring Dane Swan finding Australia's most talented swan. *Dale's Anatomy* was a medical drama featuring heart-throb, Dale Thomas, which could have been juxtaposed with *Ugly Benny*, featuring Ben Johnson. I tried and tried to think of a

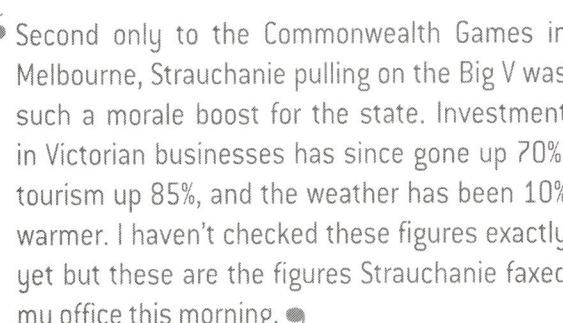

> Second only to the Commonwealth Games in Melbourne, Strauchanie pulling on the Big V was such a morale boost for the state. Investment in Victorian businesses has since gone up 70%, tourism up 85%, and the weather has been 10% warmer. I haven't checked these figures exactly yet but these are the figures Strauchanie faxed my office this morning.
>
> The Honourable STEVE BRACKS, Premier of Victoria

No way! I want Eddie to know that Bracksie knows that Strauchanie is good for business — BS

way to make Benny uglier, so it would be a more natural fit and decided upon throwing a few Horsham classics, when he wasn't looking, to get rid of that pretty face of his.

All great ideas, all ignored. This is Eddie's problem. He supposedly surrounds himself with the best talent, but when the brightest superstar comes a knockin' and a ringin', he doesn't bother responding. Disappointed, I pitched *The Burns Unit* idea to Channel 10, but they said they would only do it if they could replace Scott Burns with Andy G. I said it just wouldn't be the same. I decided to concentrate more on footy than the television, unless *Girls Of The Playboy Mansion* came on and then Strauchanie's on the couch in front of the box [television, that is].

Eddie and I never really got to have our big chat. Maybe we never will. Maybe we don't need to. CEO, Greg Swann, saw me and said that if I ever had a problem just to come and see him about it. He'll always be there. [OK, this was true when Strauchanie started writing this memoir but in fact, Swanny left the club. I asked Dale Thomas if he wanted to move in with me because Eddie told him to get out of Swanny's place but he moved in with his sister instead.]

ten

It is true that I was struggling to crack it for a game in the Collingwood seniors. It is true that Mick Malthouse and Strauchanie's relationship was strained because he took umbrage at the fact that Strauchanie insisted on checking text messages at half-time. It's OK for Mick, he doesn't get many text messages, maybe five in a busy week, whereas Strauchanie gets closer to 1000 a day. It is true that I asked Christi Malthouse out on a hot date in the hope of repairing relations with her father. OK, what started as a devious attempt to gain selection for the greatest sporting club in Australia, would sadly end in the heartbreak of the greatest sporting great this country and perhaps any other country, has produced. That is where the truth ends and the lies begin.

Strauchanie walked into the Channel 10 studios with a spring in his step, like Mal Waldon on a big news day. I felt like I was already part of the network, considering how many hours I had spent on the Big Brother website watching the housemates showering. I missed nine training sessions because I slept through my alarm after watching Krystal bathe. She was my favourite, a real natural beauty. But the only real Krystal that was on my mind was the krystal ring I might one day put on Christi Malthouse's finger, on one proviso. That her dad was still coaching Collingwood.

As it turned out, Christi was just as keen as Strauchanie to share a coffee. After my idea for the both of us to head to the Lexus Centre [on the off-chance that we might bump into Mick] was rejected, we found a cafe where we sat, drank coffee and ate cake [actually Christi refrained from eating cake because she had to read the sport that night on telly, after Quarters rang in sick with a migraine]. We spoke about everything: life, love and football and, more importantly, what Mick thought about life, love and football. The chemistry between us was amazing. Things were quickly hotting up. Weatherman Mike Larkan was nearby and I suggested to him that he may want to declare a total fire ban because there was a real heatwave coming across this city. He said it doesn't work like that. I asked him to send us a cheerio during that night's weather, he said, 'No, I am not allowed to do that.' It was awkward and then I walked away.

For the next few days Christi and Strauchanie were inseparable. I took her to see *Herbie Fully Loaded* and she took me shopping. Strauchanie was the perfect gentleman, covering all the petrol money and allowing Christi to buy the movie tickets and the popcorn and drinks from the candy bar. It wasn't until after one perfect date when Strauchanie dropped Christi off that things went pear-shaped. Christi was keen for Strauchanie to come up for a coffee. Strauchanie was keen to come up for a coffee. It was ideal: have a coffee, bump into Mick in the kitchen and start talking footy, then, hey presto, look who's lining up at centre half-forward against the Dockers that Saturday – Strauchanie! But just as every AFL coach knows, things don't always go to plan. Christi dropped the bombshell that busted open Strauchanie's heart like a piñata, but, unfortunately, there were no lollies that fell from Strauchanie's insides, just heartache and anger. These were the words Christi said that no man who's dating his footy coach's daughter, just to get a game, should ever have to hear:

'I don't live with my dad.'

Do you remember where you were when that guy from Pearl Jam committed suicide? Do you remember where you were when the Princess of Wales was killed by the Queen? Well, I remember where I was when Christi Malthouse told me she no longer lived with her father, Collingwood coach Mick Malthouse ... I was in my car sitting next to Christi Malthouse. Her words echoed like a gunshot at close range, rearranging my face with disbelief. I hadn't been lied to like this since one of the kids at school told little Strauchanie that my Speak and Spell was made out of lolly: I chipped a tooth. I broke up with Christi there and then, accusing her of emotional treason, which in some countries is a hanging offence. She was understandably upset, who wouldn't be? She probably had the whole wedding planned in that pretty little sports-reading, boundary-riding head of hers.

Do you mean Nirvana? Whatever – BS

Check facts!

Christi may well have been heartbroken, as she tried to stop fantasising about her big day in white. But Strauchanie was also fantasising about his big day in black and white. From that day on, I focussed all my energy on getting a game for the Pies. I changed my lifestyle. I went from drinking Coke to Coke Zero. I started eating Four 'n' Twenty traveller pies instead of the normal ones. That way, whenever I was having a pie, I was also burning calories by being on the move. I stopped having my nightly tub of ice-cream in front of *The Biggest Loser*. In short, I was becoming the best Strauchanie I could be. There is no bigger shame than wasted talent. Imagine if Jesus came down from the skies and decided he couldn't be arsed feeding the five thousand, or he was too busy playing his Playstation to perform any miracles. Mind you, having the highest score on Grand Theft Auto is not a miracle, it's a bloody good achievement, and Strauchanie smokes Chris Egan every time I get on it, especially at San Andreas, but you have to keep these things in perspective.

Everybody around the club noticed the difference in Strauchanie. Shane O'Bree said I was the hardest worker at the club. Lica was in awe of me on the track. Jimmy said that he'd thought it was stuff of legend, but that now he had truly seen the 'eye of the tiger'. But guess who noticed it more than anyone? Mick Malthouse. So much so that when the team sheet came out for the biggest game of the year against Sydney in Sydney, guess who was named on the wing? Strauchanie! Who would have thought that devoting time to football and not the coach's daughter would pay such big dividends?

❝ The AFL is investigating the reasons why the Collingwood Football Club refuses to play Strauchanie. We believe it to be for the good of the game that BK Strauchan plays ASAP. Never before have we seen a player claim greatness like a birth right like Strauchanie has, and we're really keen to find out if there's any substance behind all the hype. We hope there is. ❞

ANDREW DEMETRIOU, AFL Chief Executive

Would prefer you left this quote out until I have had confirmed its accuracy with Mr Demetriou.

The scene was set, the AFL were rapt. Could Strauchanie be the key that would open up the entire Sydney market? Plugger Lockett had been gone for a while now and no offence intended, but you can hardly expect Jarred Crouch to capture the hearts and minds of Sydneysiders. In the harbour city they love a little bit of Hollywood, and Strauchanie was as Hollywood as Hollywood on the Gold Coast. The good news for Strauchanie was that it was Round 12, still plenty of time to take Charlie home at the end of the year. I did the sums on the flight up. Ten rounds, three votes each, equals thirty votes. Geez, with those sorts of numbers, I could probably afford to fade out of a couple of games. But then ... another scandal.

Strauchanie gets locked in the stairwell of Stadium Australia after forgetting his pass. There is no mobile reception and Strauchanie misses the big game, surviving only on lemon chicken and a fierce determination to overcome the odds. They found me thirty-five minutes later.

Strauchanie has been cursed by that ground. The next year, Strauchanie misses the game again whilst getting clobbered around the ears for accidentally writing his hotel breakfast order on the back of our game plan. Is it that important? I don't even read the game plans and I am pretty sure if Strauchanie doesn't read the game plans, then Paul Roos doesn't read them either. Mick saw it otherwise and, as much as I tried to pin the blame on Lica and Pebbles, it looked like Strauchanie was going to have to take the rap for that one. We went on to lose by less than a goal. Mick still blames me, but in my mind, he was out-coached.

Not long after this, Strauchanie finds out he is adopted [see Chapter 8, 'Before Angelina']. My Chinese mother, Soy Bean, the woman who breastfed me, spoonfed me and then chopstick fed me, was not actually my natural mother. How could this be true? My world had been tipped upside-down, and was making me dizzy. Whenever I looked in the mirror to do my arm curls, I barely recognised myself. Did this mean I could no longer qualify for the All Asian AFL Team of the Year? Who was going to challenge Peter Bell for the captaincy now? I was confused, and that's when I started thinking of Christi again. She was the love of Strauchanie's life, I needed her back, and I would do anything to make that happen.

This is a Valentine's Day Message that Strauchanie put in the paper for Christi after we split up.

CHRISTI
Beautiful you are very,
Better than Tiffany Cherry.
In my heart you will linger,
Like the smell after someone pulls your finger.
Destiny will bring us back together,
But for the moment, is it OK if I have a crack at Heather?
[she works at the newsagent]
Love Bryan (strau, strau)

'Anything' meant accepting an invitation to McDreamy Holland's BBQ at the end of the year. McDreamy, Dids, Maxy Kleiman were there, along with Sarita Stella, Christi and some other lovely lady types. Christi's flirting with Strauchanie was outrageous. I had to take five to speak to the boys and it was unanimous, Strauchanie was in like Lara Flynn Boyle. Then, another scandal. Honestly, I wouldn't be surprised if Strauchanie is the Latin word for 'scandal'.

So, at the BBQ, Strauchanie sends a kilo package Werribee bound, but the bloody thing won't flush. I don't want to offend Brodie, so I call for Sarita to come in and help me out. She had never seen anything like it, then, lo and behold, Brodie walks past, followed by Christi. Everyone catches Strauchanie and Sarita in the can together, trying to get rid of the BS mess but that was nothing compared to the mess it created.

McDreamy's screaming at Strauchanie, 'Get out of my house!' Sarita is crying at Brodie, 'Nothing happened!' Christi is yelling at Sarita, 'How could you do this?' Dids starts screaming at Brodie, 'Why didn't you handball to me in Round 5?' Strauchanie is pretty good at reading people, so he thought to himself, it's time to leave, not just the BBQ, but the football club altogether.

All my attempts to leave the club ended badly. Strauchanie even spilt a drug test sample on a freshly signed contract with the Western Bulldogs. So Strauchanie always finds himself back at the Pies, back where he belongs. If Smorgy's is Strauchanie's spiritual home, then the Lexus Centre would probably be his spiritual beach house. [See

Chapter 12 'It's Nice to be Wanted' for Strauchanie's exposé on the poaching tactics of all the other clubs.]

It didn't take long, however, for more sand to be kicked in Strauchanie's face when he tried to get back with Christi and she dropped another bombshell ... she was engaged to be married! Strauchanie hadn't been hit in the guts like that since Spazz Dooley hit Strauchanie in the guts for stealing his Easter egg. My life had yet again been turned on its head, like Strauchanie descending from a specky. I didn't even know Christi was seeing anybody. True, Shannon Cox had approached me and requested my permission to ask Christi out. I gave him my blessing only because I knew he didn't stand a chance. This engaged thing was shocking. I had always thought she would wait for me. Christi is still the only woman I have ever considered buying a box of Cadbury Roses for. She will always be special to Strauchanie. She will always ride the boundary line of my heart.

A MONUMENT TO THE GAME

CHAPTER ELEVEN ->

eleven

Horsham is a great town. It's my town. Strauchanietown. I wouldn't be surprised if they do call it Strauchanietown, one day. They can change a street name in Melbourne to AC/DC Lane, so, why not? What did that band ever do anyway? They're not even original. Their stuff sounds exactly like that band Acker Dacker. Now that Strauchanie has hit the big time, Horsham has come calling. Didn't take long for the wolves to circle. The Mayor rang me and wanted to arrange a meeting. Luckily, I get back to Horsham regularly to see my family and pay off a few debts, so they meetings haven't put me out too much.

Before I go any further, let me just give you a bit of background on Horsham. Horsham is a country town in north-west Victoria, 300 km from Melbourne [about a 72-dim sim trip]. The town of Horsham has a population of about 13 000 [about the size of an NRL crowd, but with more necks]. Many locals were worried about the bad luck that would come from having the number '13' on the town's population sign. Their fears proved to be well-founded when a young Strauchanie smashed into the sign while riding his bike many years ago. Ironically, I lost 13 teeth in the collision. Fortunately, they were only those lolly teeth. A wombat grabbed them and ran off. He's probably a big hit, right now, back in his burrow. The other wombats will be going, 'Put the teeth in, Kev, put the funny teeth in!' Kev will be dancing around and waving his arms with the funny teeth in … um … where was I? Oh, yeah. What else can I tell you about Horsham? It's on the Wimmera River which is stacked with an abundance of fish. Well, it was, until Strauchanie entered the annual Labour Day fishing competition. How was I to know that the use of dynamite wasn't within the rules? I was subsequently disqualified when some of the dynamite I threw into the river just happened accidentally to land in the boat of the defending champion, Gary Westcott. Fortunately, Gary dived into the water just before his boat blew up. Being nearby, Strauchanie thought he'd better pick him up in his boat. I couldn't see Gary, but I felt the bottom of my boat hit what I assumed was a floating log, so I took the boat back into shore to assess the damage.

Don't get me wrong, Strauchanie's a big fan of fishing. It's a great Australian pastime and an ideal way to relax. For example, one day, after training, Dane Swan walked into the Lexus Centre holding a huge whiting, saying he had just caught it the Yarra, and that a whole school of them were still there for the taking. Lica had a fishing rod in his boot and was happy to lend it to me, so I headed down and dropped a line in. I was there for an hour, and not a bite. By that stage, a number of the boys were watching from the Lexus Centre and giving me a bit of curry. I came back and said to Dane Swan, 'What's the story? I haven't caught a thing.'

Dane reluctantly let me in on a little secret. 'All right, Strauchanie, I'll give you a bit of a tip. You need to use these Guy Richards badges from the merchandise shop as bait. The fish are attracted to the silver backing when it sparkles in the water.'

'Sure thing,' I replied and away I went.

I was sitting there for another hour, and still nothing, but the waiting gave me some time to think about how Guy Richards should have an endless supply of nicknames. I mean, you think about it. 'Lou' as in Lou Richards, the famous Collingwood ruckman. 'Keith' Richards ... 'Denise' Richards. Put it this way, there'd be enough for a different name for each day of the week. I decided to start first thing the next morning, when he'd be known as 'Cliff' Richards, followed by 'King Richards the Third' – Strauchanie was on fire!

After a couple of hours fishing, catching nothing and missing a team meeting, I returned and found Dane doing arm curls in the gym. I launched straight into my favourite made-up song, 'Dane, you're not a Swan, you're a Magpie!'

Shane O'Bree was nearby and loved it. I recorded it for him for another ringtone. Obi could release an album of Strauchanie classics. May have to keep an eye on that one.

Dane looked at me. 'What do you want, Strauchanie?'

I explained to him that his plan for Strauchanie to catch fish was riddled with problems, and that not one fish had been caught.

Dane looked perplexed. 'You actually tried it? Oh, Strauchanie...' He continued with his curls.

Strauchanie did the only thing I could think of. 'Dane, you're not a Swan, you're a Magpie!'

I arrived at the Horsham municipal offices for my meeting with the mayor, but was told to sit and wait in the foyer area. I said to the girl behind the counter, 'You do know who I am, don't you?'

'Bryan Strauchan,' she replied.

'Ah, you've been following my progress, have you?'

'No, you've got 35 outstanding parking fines. There's a picture of you up on the wall.'

Strauchanie's brain immediately went into 'hang on, there might be a clever way to get out of this one, if I can think of something quickly' mode. 'What if I sign that picture of me for you? Will that make those fines fall into the bin, never to be seen again?' Strauchanie sheepishly asked, tapping the side of my nose with my finger.

She was unmoved. Time to bring in the back-up Strauchanie emergency plan. 'You are the most beautiful woman I've ever seen. You're the complete package with your boobs and other stuff ... um ... who do I make the cheque out to?'

The mayor stuck his head out of his office and gestured for me to come in. He offered me a water and asked me to sit down ... but Strauchanie's a busy man, 'Cut the crap, Mayor,' I said. 'What do you want?'

'Strauchanie, my son's primary school is having a fete and I was wondering if you could make an appearance?'

'That's it?'

'Yeah ...'

'Will I be like the 'King of the Fete' in a robe and a crown? Will there be a parade?'

'No, the idea was for you just to turn up and mingle. It's a pretty small affair.'

'Well, Strauchanie doesn't get out of bed for less than 10 000 people!'

'The fete goes all day, so you can pick the time you want to turn up, and we can make it as quick as possible. I just assumed you'd want to put something back into the community that served you so well as a youngster. Are you sure you don't want to think about it?'

'Will there be fairy floss?'

'Yes.'

'Strauchanie's in!'

Just then, there's a knock at the door and in strolls Sydney player and ex-Horsham lad himself, Adam Goodes.

> Strauchanie is the biggest name in Horsham. Every-body wants a piece of him, mainly because he owes a lot of people money. I have had to put a block on his number on my phone because he kept calling me in the middle of the night screaming 'Brown-how?' I think he may have been under the influence.
>
> ADAM GOODES, Dual Brownlow medallist and Sydney Swans champion

The mayor jumps out of his seat, over his table and gives Goodesy the sort of grovelling welcome you'd expect for an international dignitary. I'm thinking, he's not Nelson Mandela or Mother Teresa or Grant Denyer. It's Adam Bloody Goodes.

I then had to sit through 20 boring minutes of them telling each other how good they were.

'Oh Goodesy, two whole Brownlows – what an achievement!'

'Oh, Mayor, two Tidy Towns – what an achievement!'

'Oh, Goodesy, you're so talented.'

'Oh, Mayor, you're so incorruptible and morally upright.'

Strauchanie had heard enough. 'Why don't you two get a room?'

As it turned out, Goodesy did have a room. They were putting him up in the swankiest hotel in Horsham. Seriously, if they're making Goodesy 'King of the Fete' then I'm outta here!

The mayor eventually got around to the reason he wanted to see Goodesy. Get this, right. No appearance for Goodesy at some two-bit, half-arsed fete. No! Goodesy is having a new junior community sporting facility named after him. Can you believe it? The Adam Goodes Junior Sports Complex. Sure, he's won two Brownlows and a premiership, but Strauchanie, potentially, could double that before his career is over. How stupid would they look then? The town really hadn't thought this through. They needed to acknowledge Strauchanie's achievements, at the very least to save face, and I thought I might know how.

What's in Strauchanie's footy bag?

FOOTY BOOTS – Strauchanie knew that these were the boots for him when he saw them on special in the Rebel Sport mid-year catalogue. A number of manufacturers did approach me in the hope that I would wear and endorse their brands but they wouldn't come to the party on my request to be put on their board of directors.

FOOTY SOCKS – Strauchanie's lucky footy socks. I've never lost a game in them. Sure, I'm yet to play a game in them but boy have I trained the house down in them. I refuse to wash them as I'm afraid I'll wash away the good luck. It also makes it easier to find my bag by simply following the smell.

FOOTY SHORTS – My team mates try to poke fun at me because the tag in my shorts says size XXXL. They don't realise that they're that big in order to accommodate me in the front. Bucks' may be on a good package but Strauchanie came with a good package.

MP3 PLAYER – Some players like to psych themselves up before a game by listening to music. I don't. I just walk around with the earphones in so that no-one else talks to me.

TOWEL – A good towel should be selected on its suitability to flick team mates on the bum with. I got Travis Cloke an absolute beauty on the left butt cheek after training once. The noise of the whack could be heard on the other side of the Yarra River. It may explain why Trav favours the right butt cheek when kicking for goal. Next time he shanks one, read his lips – he definitely says "#@*%*# Strauchanie!"

A CONTAINER OF LEFTOVER LEMON CHICKEN – Sustenance.

PRE – SIGNED PHOTOS OF STRAUCHANIE – To save me potentially getting mugged, I simply carry a wad of these and just toss them out of the car window as I drive away from the ground.

I was back that afternoon for another meeting with the mayor. This time I was armed with some rough plans I had knocked up over lunch. As I burst into his office, I put one hand up to silence him before he could speak and, without missing a beat, I hit him with my idea. 'Mayor, I've got three words for you – the Big Strauchanie.' The stunned look on his face was enough for me to think, Strauchanie – you've blown him away with this one. 'I'm telling you, Mayor, the Big Strauchanie is going to put Horsham on the map. Just as the Big Banana has done for Coffs Harbour, the Big Merino for Goulburn and the Big Rock for Alice Springs.' [I still can't believe the size of the Big Rock. It must've taken them ages to build it. And another thing, they let all those people climb it. It's only matter of time before someone falls straight through that fibreglass roof.] Anyway, it was time to lay my plans out on the mayor's desk. As I said earlier, the plans were drawn up by me, at lunchtime, on some napkins from the cafe I was dining in. 'As you can see, Mayor, the Big Strauchanie is an exact replica of me, but bigger. In fact, it's a whopping 20-metres worth of Strauchanie. That's not a big birthmark, by the way, it's just some tomato sauce.'

By now the Mayor is shaking his head and smiling, presumably in amazement. Strauchanie had put a lot of thought into this, in between the main course and dessert. For instance, visitors to the Big Strauchanie would actually enter via a lift that goes straight up my shorts [a bonus for the lady tourists] and all the way to the viewing platform, where they can look out through my eyes. That's the great thing about it. People can actually do what footballers have been trying to do for years – get into Strauchanie's head. They'd be happy to pay for that privilege. In fact, what's the bet Kevin Sheedy's the first person up there?

The mayor sat back in contemplation and put his hands on his head and then took another close look at my drawings.

'Is that a door where your bum is?'

'Yep. That's the emergency exit.'

'Look, it's a pretty ambitious project, Strauchanie. It won't be cheap to operate. How do you ensure a regular cash flow?'

'Easy. It pays for itself. See that football spinning on Big Strauchanie's finger? That's a revolving restaurant.'

'It ain't gonna happen, Strauchanie.'

I couldn't believe he was prepared to let one of the great modern marvels of this century just slip through his fingers like that. I'd even done a bare-bones budget costing, which involved each class at the local primary school making a different Strauchanie body part out of papier-maché. We simply truck the individual parts to the proposed area and assemble the Big Strauchanie on-site. They might need to build a huge carport to protect it from the weather but otherwise, it's a no-brainer.

The mayor was proving to be more difficult to convince than I first thought. As I suspected, it came down to him playing favourites. I wasn't going to let him get away with it. Strauchanie had to expose the mayor for what he really stood for. Strauchanie knew, deep down, that the real reason the Big Strauchanie wouldn't go ahead was because the

A MONUMENT TO THE GAME

'I worship the ground Goodesy walks on' mayor was putting all of his weight and power behind the Adam Goodes Junior Sports Shed thingo. If that was the case, Strauchanie was going to be very, very, very disappointed. And insulted, quite frankly.

The mayor was happy to continue trying to pull the wool over Strauchanie's eyes. 'Listen, Strauchanie, yes, we have already committed a large sum of council and public money to the building of the Adam Goodes Junior Sports Complex, but that has been in the planning for a number of years. Adam has had a remarkable football career, including numerous noteworthy highlights and special achievements. He's been a great ambassador for this city, his club and football in general and deserves any recognition that comes his way.'

Strauchanie wasn't going to let this go. 'I tell you what, Mayor, Strauchanie can solve your dilemma for you. Why not combine both ideas and honour Horsham's two football superstars together? Picture this. You're driving towards Horsham. You're approaching the sign that says: "Welcome to Horsham". You look up, pull your car over to the side of the road and gasp as you wind down your window. There, right before your very eyes, is one of the most amazing things you've ever seen – the Big Strauchanie taking a specky over the Big Goodesy.'

'Get out!'

CHAPTER TWELVE—>

twelve

One of the advantages of being a legend in the making is that everybody wants a slice of Strauchan-lova. [Get it? It's a clever take on Pavlova] I have had every club in the AFL enquire about my services at one time or another. Although, it's true, the West Coast call was taken by Mum at 3 am and she dutifully told them that there was no Charlie living there, only a Bryan and a Roy. They blew a whistle and hung up. I thought it may be fun and informative for Strauchanie to blast open the locker room doors and tell you how your team tried to lure the great man into their club colours.

Adelaide
Great club, great jumper, especially considering the gay pride message. I applaud that. Neil Craig rang me on a Tuesday night. Strauchanie didn't take his call. I wasn't playing hard to get but I was watching *Two And A Half Men* and no-one interrupts Strauchanie when he is watching *Two And A Half Men*. I once made Scott Burns and Shane Wakelin wait outside in their car for ten minutes because the episode

wasn't over. It was worth getting yelled at by Mick at training. He just doesn't understand the genius that is Jon Cryer. I eventually returned Neil's call on Friday morning. We made some small chat, he shared his vision for the future of football and I made some killer jokes about Graham Johncock's name. 'You see, Neil, "john" is another name for toilet and "cock" is another name for "willy".' He has a very quiet laugh but he appreciated it. We spoke for a while and he was very interested. I told him he would have to trade big and that wasn't code for trading Rhett Biglands. Oh, no, Rhett's too small fry when you're talking about water this deep. Neil was open and honest and told me he was prepared to trade Brownlow medallist Andrew McLeod, smart on-baller Simon Goodwin and Tyson Edwards. Strauchanie suggested he throw in a first-round draft pick just to get the deal across the line. Neil made a noise that I took to be 'right on Strauchanie!' So, there Strauchanie is, about to sign on the dotted line, when I see the news: Mark Ricciuto has scurvy. I couldn't believe it, who gets scurvy these days? Apparently some doctor named Ross River diagnosed him. Strauchanie promptly rings Neil Craig and says, 'Strauchanie's body is a temple, I can't risk getting scurvy and turning yellow. How would that look at Boutique?' I quickly hung up and I never spoke to him again. OK, that's not quite true. After a few beers at Shane Wakelin's house, I rang Craigy at 1 am and yelled down the phone, 'Johncock' before hanging up ... I'm pretty sure he didn't know it was Strauchanie.

PAGE 125:

Andrew McLeod has <u>not</u> won a Brownlow. Well, Strauchanie wins a! So I bet Crows really spewing.

Brisbane

Jonathan Brown once took me aside and said, 'Strauchanie, how do you do it? You're a freak. I look at you and think, how does this guy play AFL football?' Wow, what a compliment. In my book, Jonathan Brown is Leigh Matthews' natural successor in the Divine Homes commercials and that is about as big a compliment as Strauchanie can give. Vossy tried to get me to Brisbane once, but Strauchanie took the opportunity to make jokes about Jed Adcock's name ... [I'll give you a second to get it, Strauchanie had to explain it to Anthony Rocca.] I wasn't particularly interested in joining the Lions, so in the end I didn't.

I remember the first time I met Strauchanie was in the Lions change rooms just after we knocked the Pies off in a big game. I have no idea how he got in there, dressed in his Collingwood tracksuit, but he walked up to me, eyeballed me and said, 'You, me, Hird, Roo, Woey and maybe Crawf . . . Brownlow Cafe!' I was a bit taken aback and I mentioned to him that he had actually never won a Brownlow. Before I had a chance to blink, Strauchanie tipped a bottle of blue Gatorade over me and stormed out. I would have decked him but I was icing my quad at the time. Strauchanie is a very complex unit.

MICHAEL VOSS, Brownlow medallist and three-time premiership captain of the Brisbane Lions

Carlton

I once visited an abandoned warehouse they called Optus Oval – seriously, I wouldn't dump a body in that joint. Strauchanie had to let one rip just to freshen the place up a bit. Luckily, Ryan Houlihan walked in and I blamed it on him. He protested his innocence to which Strauchanie hit back, 'You smelt it, you dealt it! You whiffed it, you piffed it! You copped it, you dropped it!' There is no comeback against such logic, so poor old Ryan left the room deflated and defeated. The Blues have a billionaire in charge now and nothing seems to have changed. I imagine he doesn't use the facilities, I imagine he hightails it back to his own joint when he feels his bowel do a bit of circle work. The Carlton boys treated me well. It was great to meet Setanta, I was a big fan, especially of that song he did with Rob Thomas. Nick Stevens seemed like a nice fella and strike Strauchanie blind if it wasn't like looking into a mirror. Kouta was also a lovely chap, I spoke slowly so he understood me and that seemed to work. I also sat down and spoke to Lance Whitnall over a couple of Krispy Kremes and had a chat about where we saw the Blues going. I said they're going nowhere in a hurry, then Ryan Houlihan walked past, I cut one and quickly left.

Essendon

The message from Strauchanie was clear. Get rid of Jimmy Hird 'All-About-It' and Matty 'The Bacardi Breezer Geezer' Lloyd and I'd consider coming down to Windy Hill. Although I had concerns about training at Windy Hill. I mean how

Windy does it get? Strauchanie's hair is a masterpiece held together by salon wax and Deep Heat, but if it's blowing a Brendon Gale then who knows what could happen? Strauchanie only wants to worry about taking speckies and kicking unkickable goals. I do not want to be thinking about my fringe, that's my opponent's job. Sheedy wasn't impressed with my views, nor was he impressed when I made jokes about Jason Winderlich's name. Sheeds said he thought I overrated myself as a footballer. I told him to 'Winderlich my arse and would he want Monfries with that serve?' He told Strauchanie to grow up and we haven't spoken since.

Fremantle

Had a big tilt at Strauchanie. The whole coaching staff came over and made an impressive presentation. Again it came down to finding the right trades. Can you imagine Strauchanie playing in the same forward line as Pavlova? I can't. I need space. Space to lead into, space to take speckies, space to do goal celebrations. I once berated Ben Johnson for interrupting a goal celebration I was doing at training. It was a cartwheel, into a duck-dive, a quick robot dance followed by a second duck-dive, then up to my knees to finish with jazz hands. It was bulletproof, until Johnno nailed me with a 40-metre pass. I went ballistic. 'How dare you interrupt my goal celebration? Call yourself a leader? Leading us down the garden path it seems, don't ever cross me again, Johnno!' He tried to explain that we were doing circle work and we weren't suppose to be kicking goals, let

IT'S NICE TO BE WANTED

alone taking three minutes to celebrate them. I put my arm around him and explained, 'If Strauchanie's not allowed to kick goals, then Strauchanie's hitting the showers!' But back to Freo. Chris Connolly is a professional AFL coach, he recognised Strauchanie's natural ability early. Medibank [Paul Medhurst] always tells me Connolly used to bang on about Strauchanie in his pre-game speeches to the players. Taz tells me the coach is still obsessed by me. What started as a coach admiring and fantasising about an opposition player has become a little bit creepy. I respect the man, but for my own safety, and for Chris's own mental health, I think it's best that Strauchanie keeps his distance.

Geelong

The Cats made a huge play for Strauchanie, even going to the length of getting Balmey down to 'Not-so' Skilled Stadium. I can't lie. I was shattered when I was told that 'Fine And' Balmey was leaving Collingwood. I rang him and told him that I was outraged and that no-one should put up with that and that I was going to walk, nobody treats Strauchanie's mates like that and gets away with it. In the end, I stayed. I was tired and it seemed like an awful lot of trouble to go to.

Hawthorn

Brown and gold? Maybe at a fancy-dress party if the theme was 'Poo And Wee', but I hardly think those colours are conducive to Strauchanie getting 100 per cent out of himself.

Crawf and I caught up at a footy skills clinic, and he was pretty keen to get Strauchanie to Glenferrie. I pitched to him my idea of the Brownlow Cafe, where it's Strauchanie, Bucks, Vossy, Juddy, Goodesy, Crawf and Mark Ricciuto serving the customers. Imagine getting your burger and fries from Shane Crawford! 'Oops, I forgot your Coke, here comes Strauchanie!' He wasn't into the idea, in fact, I think he called me a dickhead. I eased the tension by making some 3-vote gags about Ben Dixon's surname and left.

Half way!

Kangaroos

Dean Laidley rang me to gauge Strauchanie's interest in becoming a Roo. I didn't have the heart to tell him that I would rather chafe myself into an early grave than play for the cash-strapped Kangas. Strauchanie is an elite AFL player and he needs to be cashed up, and that was never going to happen at Arden Street. I checked out the facilities and, fair dinkum, I wouldn't hold Spazz Dooley's 21st there, let alone expect to get the best out of myself. Don't get me wrong, I admire the shinboner spirit, but at the time of Dean's approach, there were three blokes named Shannon at the club [Grant, Motlop and Watt]. What next, Glenn Archer changes his name to Kylie? In the end, I couldn't tell Dean I had zero interest in crossing over, so I did the only thing I could think of, I lowered my voice and pretended to be Guy Richards. Dean hung up and it's never come up again.

Melbourne
Strauchanie had very fruitful conversations with the Reverend, Neale Daniher. Strauchanie was up front with the supercoach. 'Reverend, how would you like a brand new altar boy under your belt?' Unfortunately, Neale misunderstood me and asked me never to call him again. I later found out that Neale actually had me on speaker phone and was entertaining his local parish priest with Mrs Daniher, a clergyman and Cameron Bruce. We sorted it all out, cleared up the misunderstanding and Neale was keen to talk shop with Strauchanie. We quickly organised a deal: Robertson, White, Davey Train and Brock McLean to the Pies, BS to the Dees. It fell apart when Neale asked Strauchanie to do a drug test. Strauchanie responded, 'How about you do a test Neale? How about you do a "Miss Out on a Future Brownlow Medallist Test"? Guess what, Neale? You passed with flying colours!' And like Craig David, Strauchanie walked away. I've only spoken to Neale once since, when I rang him to suggest he give Matthew Bate the nickname 'Master' ... Neale paused and reminded me not to call him at home, I was on speaker phone again and Father O'Brien was not impressed.

Port Power
Choco Williams asked me down to Alberton Oval to train, and Strauchanie trained the house down. The Burgoynes were looking at me thinking, 'I've never seen a white man with so much pace, he's like Josh Francou with a turbo engine and that's before he had his legs amputated'. I could hear

IT'S NICE TO BE WANTED

Tredrea thinking, 'This bloke is the genuine article, the real deal, the best chip in the packet. We need him in our team if we are seriously going to call ourselves the Power'. In the end, Strauchanie figured if he could catch scurvy playing for the Crows he could catch it playing for the Power. I made a joke about Brendan Lade's surname and told Choco, thanks but no thanks.

Richmond

The Tigers have never officially approached Strauchanie, which, in my mind, exposes them as naive and out of touch. Maybe Terry has spent too long in the solarium and his brain has been fried but, fair dinkum, imagine if you were a lifelong Tigers fan and you're reading this and you're finding out that your club did not go after the greatest unplayed player in the history of the VFL/AFL, yet they go after Nathan Brown who was always going to break his leg in horrific circumstances. Anyone who knows anything about football knew that was going to happen. Strauchanie calls Terry Wallace and the Richmond recruiting staff 'Jim and Phil' ... because they're crackers!

St Kilda

Strauchanie nearly marched his way down to St Kilda at the request of president Rod Butters 'Up'. He invited me to his house, which I estimated to be four times the size of the Lexus Centre. In fact, Strauchanie swears he saw a Lexus parked in one of the spare bedrooms. I certainly felt less guilty knocking off a variety of shampoos and ties, knowing that this bloke is as loaded as Microsoft. Strauchanie demanded an end to the rotating captaincy policy. I mean, if it kept on going, Troy Schwarze would one day lead the Saints out, and that could not happen on Strauchanie's watch. It was tempting to join the Saints. I like the way Robert Harvey 'Norman' goes about it. When I am in my early sixties, I hope I am still running around like him. [Probably I'll still be winning Brownlows. Strauchanie will probably end up like the Pope: I'll just serve until I die. Probably cark it on the boundary line, after kicking the miraculous match-winning goal to win another grand final for the Pies. Strauchanie may be the first bloke to win the Norm Smith posthumously. What a fitting end to a glittering career!] In the end, the St Kilda deal could not get done. Message to Andrew Demetriou from Strauchanie: bring on free agency ASAP!

IT'S NICE TO BE WANTED

Sydney Swans
No thanks. Don't like the infrastructure. Not of the club, but of the city itself. If Paul Roos wants Strauchanie, he is going to have to get on the blower to Premier Morris Iemma and Lord Mayor Clover Moore and get that city into shape. The traffic is as unbearable as Hawthorn's game plan, or Spazz Dooley's attempts at the Horsham Primary School's spelling bee.

Western Bulldogs:
Oh, so close. After the Brodie–Sarita–Christi scandal, I was close to joining the Bulldogs. In fact, to become an official Bulldog, all I had to do was pass a drug test. Lindsay Gilbee would be Magpie bound as a result of Strauchanie wizzing into a cup. But the results created the biggest controversy in the AFL since Mark Porter left Carlton and joined the Kangaroos. Strauchanie had tested positive ... to MSG. I had just knocked off a platefull of Mum's famous lemon chicken and, admittedly, Strauchanie had been buzzing like a blowie on ice. Rocket 'Blast Off' Eade was shocked, yet understandably supportive. He said the door would always be open at the smelly, abandoned warehouse they call their 'home ground'.

West Coast Eagles

> PAGE 135:
> Bryan, lawyers said this whole entry on West Coast must go! And before you ask again, your 'A Few Good Men' defence will <u>not</u> work this time! Guess who really can't handle the truth!

This section was deemed defamatory by the publisher as it could lead to the arrests of almost every member of the West Coast Eagles playing group and off-field staff from 1996 through to 2007 [if claims by Strauchanie are true]. However, Strauchanie is 'permitted to let it be known that, as a part of discussions Bryan Strauchan had with Eagles coach John Worsfold, he was heard to have made several jokes about Dean Cox'.

In the end, of course, Strauchanie stayed at Collingwood after they promised to pay some outstanding parking fines. 'Typical,' I told Mick Malthouse. 'Even Strauchanie's parking fines are outstanding'. He shook his head, grunted and walked away ... in agreement.

CHAPTER THIRTEEN→

thirteen

When I go back to my home town, nowadays, I am deeply saddened to see young boys running around on parched turf, unfit for playing on. The future stars of this game deserve much more than dirt and dust. Last time I was in Horsham I sat down with local senior coach Graham 'Goldie' Lane who could only raise his hands in the air in despair. He was adamant that the blame lay fairly and squarely with El Nino. I said: 'Well, maybe you shouldn't have drafted him in the first place.' Why would you go to South America looking for players anyway? I mean, how many are currently contracted at AFL level? Not many. How many would even know how to play the game? I can only think of one, Harry O'Brien, who's from Brazil. Harry's one of a kind. A special breed. He spent his childhood training in the high altitudes of the Andes, living amongst alpacas. Clever kid, Harry 'coz alpacas are renowned for being able to kick with all four feet. The only other South American connection Strauchanie

Bryan, the Andes are <u>not</u> in Brazil!

Well, where are the Alpacas? - BS

THE FUTURE OF FOOTBALL

knows of was in the 1960s. My uncle Gavin, or 'Gav 1, 2 and 3', as the family calls him due to his multiple personalities, often recounts the story of how Essendon secretly managed to sign famed revolutionary, Che Guevara. At the time they were looking for a good, hard, in-and-under type and Che fitted the bill. Unfortunately, Che's VFL adventure didn't eventuate as his football dream was cut short by the career-ending injury of being shot and killed. Uncle Gav's theory was that the Bombers had no chance of getting Che Guevara, and they merely did the deal as part of a ploy to draft his son, Che Cockatoo-Collins, under the father-son rule. Uncles Gav 1 and 3 haven't been seen since he escaped from the treatment centre. Gav 2 has left a few messages on my answering machine.

There's talk of all this money being directed into grassroots football at the moment, but right now, due to the drought, at the grassroots, the grass is … well … rooted … and Strauchanie doesn't use the word 'rooted' lightly. I've probably used it three times in my whole life. There was one time, in Year 9, when we had to give our assessment on another classmate's woodwork project. Jimmy Hamapopoulous made a pencil case that looked like an elephant had sat on it. Strauchanie's assessment:

❝ Strauchanie emailed me the morning of the Victory Grand Final and he just said 'Never pass off'. I took that advice and the rest is history. ❞
ARCHIE THOMPSON, Striker – Melbourne Victory

'rooted'. Our woodwork teacher, Mr Kenter, said that it was inappropriate for me to utter such a word, let alone write it in red texta on Jimmy's project. The second time I used the word was when Alan Didak cleaned up Heath Scotland in the middle of the G that year. A newspaper rang me and asked for my thoughts on Alan Didak's prospects at the tribunal. Strauchanie's assessment, 'rooted'. The third time I used the word was when, listed as an emergency, once again I mistakenly wandered into the ground announcer's booth at the G. During a brief chat he asked me for my assessment of Collingwood's game plan. 'Rooted', I said, realising too late that that I had been leaning against the 'ON' button and that the question and my answer had both been broadcast to all 85 000 fans gathered at the Collingwood v Essendon Anzac Day blockbuster. Collingwood ended up winning easily that year, and when I was approached by Mick after the game, I cleverly explained to him that the PA had cut me off mid-sentence and that my completed answer was that Collingwood's game plan was 'rooted ... in genius'. Mick, for some reason, didn't buy it, and must've spent a bit of time flicking through the thesaurus because, in a frenzied verbal assault, he managed to throw a list of insults at me regarding my future that all had similar meanings to the word 'rooted'.

One solution to the turf problem facing our local clubs is obviously the installation of artificial grass. Now, before I go any further, I would just like to state that, yes, I did invest in an artificial turf company. But the company, Carpet Burn Fake Grass Pty Ltd, is in liquidation and, therefore, there is no

Bryan, Alan was cleared of any wrongdoing arising from this clash.

THE FUTURE OF FOOTBALL

conflict of interest in my comments. Unfortunately, we were ahead of our time and on the verge of exploding onto the market when our Burmese supplier, all of a sudden, decided to abscond with our money. I do still have some samples of the product in my garage, if anyone is interested in buying them. There's probably enough to do that thin strip in the middle of a driveway. Although it doesn't respond well to dripping car oil or water or sunlight, for that matter.

I can't believe it's not grass!

It's not just the substandard grounds that are of concern. These days there are plenty of things that can get in the way of a young footballer's progress. Firstly, there's the lure of non-contact sports, like soccer. Don't get me wrong.

I'm a big fan of soccer. Strauchanie sat up and watched a lot of the last World Cup. As luck would have it, I changed the channel during an ad break on *Up Late with Hotdogs* and caught the Australia versus Croatia game. Australia did well considering they had to get a guy out of the crowd to be the goalie. They could have given him a Socceroo shirt – at least!

Another sport that football is competing against for young talent is basketball. There are those who have managed to forge a career in both. Port Adelaide's Dean Brogan holds the honour of winning an NBL and AFL premiership double. Sure, it sounds impressive, but when Strauchanie's career is over, I'll have combined a few more Australian titles than that. Generations to come will be talking about Strauchanie – AFL, NBL, NRL, A-League, Bells Beach and Birdman Rally champion. Dean Brogan's greatest

THE FUTURE OF FOOTBALL

achievement, of course, was punching a Crows fan in the nose at the airport. The Crows fan asked for it by yelling out: 'You're playing for the wrong team, dickhead.' After quickly checking that he played for Port Adelaide, Dean soon worked out that the guy was having a go at him. Personally, I don't have a problem with the word 'dickhead' as long as it doesn't follow an insult. I've had people direct it at me heaps of times, but it's always been done in a positive way. 'Nice shirt, dickhead' or 'well played, dickhead' or 'your goal, dickhead!' See, it doesn't take much to say something nice about someone. I've written down all of those comments and stuck them up in my room for the rare times when I need some inspiration.

Collingwood's very own, but now de-listed, David Fanning was another to cross over from basketball to footy. I nicknamed him 'Slam Dunk', which didn't really take off. So, I expanded it to 'Slam Dunk Chip Monk'. Lica laughed in disbelief when I told him of the new extended version and he suggested I make it even longer. That Thursday at training, I've run past David Fanning for a handball yelling: 'Slam Dunk Chip Monk Living in the Top Bunk'. Lica fell over, he was laughing so much. The other boys kept telling me how brilliant they thought it was and that's when we all hatched a plan for me to write it on David's car with shaving cream. Rhyce Shaw gave me a can of shaving cream and away I went. We must have caught David on a bad day because he wasn't happy about it. In fact, he was pretty pissed off. Especially when he discovered that it wasn't shaving cream at all. It was spray paint. Rhyce had no explanation as to how the mix-up could've occurred. It cost Strauchanie four weeks wages to pay for the new paint job on David's car, but the boys are still laughing about it, so, I'd say it was worth it.

We're always being told that mums are worried about their sons getting hurt playing footy, when the truth is that it's just as dangerous walking down the street. Strauchanie's been attacked out the front of his own house on a number of occasions. Most of our neighbours aren't very friendly, to be honest. The Coopers across the road have three young boys who are nothing but trouble. One day, I was collecting my mail and I felt something hard bounce off my shoulder blade. Just as I go to grab my shoulder in pain, a rock makes an almighty 'bang!' as it thunders into the letterbox. Without hesitation, I ran across the road and found the three Cooper

---

Dear Neighbour,

Cut that bloody tree down or I will rip it out myself you bloody drongo! One more word to the local council about [insert name here] late night Jacuzzi parties and I will burn your letterbox right down to the ground you silly mofo!

Regards
Bryan "Superstar" Strauchan

boys hiding behind a car with a pile of rocks. One by one, I picked them up by their ears and gave them a Chinese burn. Not your everyday, mickey mouse, Chinese burn, I might add. A traditional family Chinese burn that has been passed down through generations of Strauchans. It dates back to the Ming dynasty and involves the use of not only your hands but your feet as well. My great-grandfather was the world's foremost master of this form of the Chinese burn, and the blueprint for this ancient technique is the most closely guarded secret in my family. It's not just about the Chinese burn. It's about disciplining your body. In the wrong hands, it could be extremely dangerous. We've also all been taught only to use the Chinese burn in self defence or during instances of road rage.

There's also the ongoing dispute I'm having with the family next-door. They know that I'm a footballer, so they should be expecting the football to make its way over the fence now and again. I casually jumped over the fence to fetch it one day, then thought to myself, maybe I should do the right thing and look in a window to see if anyone is home. Their 18-year-old part-time model daughter was in the room, getting changed. Fifteen minutes has passed and she still hasn't seen me. I eventually decide to knock on the window. She looks up as she's putting her jeans on, screams and stumbles backwards, falling over her bed. I rush in to see if she's all right and she points her hair straightener at me and says: 'Get away from me or I'll call the police.' Her boyfriend still gives me a greasy stare whenever he sees me. Little does he know that Strauchanie could take him down easily with one swing of a cricket bat, if I snuck up behind him.

So, where is football heading? Despite a long list of concerns, I think football is in safe hands. Andrew Demetriou must be doing something right. [Look at his wife. She's pretty hot. He's batting above his average there.] Let's face it, the game will still be going strong, long after you and I have gone and long after Andrew Demetriou has retired. There is, however, one group of people who will make sure that the game will flourish, and that's the fans. It is these very same people who will immortalise Strauchanie, in years to come, when the significance of the Brownlow Medal is outstripped by the Strauchanie Medal – awarded to the most talented player not given proper opportunity.

All in all, Strauchanie is quite comfortable with where the game is heading. I'm on a Jason recliner with the foot thingy out, happy to settle in. So rest assured 'coz Strauchanie thinks that the future is pretty bright and I haven't even touched on the silver spacesuit-looking outfits the players will be wearing.

CHAPTER FOURTEEN→

fourteen

Football's not just about having the skills to play the game. Like any sport, the AFL has its own jargon and terminology. Imagine trying to explain to an outsider from say, Tasmania, how our great game of Aussie Rules works, let alone what all the phrases mean. The Australian Government hasn't helped. Where are all the footy questions on their new immigrant test? Strauchanie thinks that people coming into this country should know what 'shinboner spirit' is. Every player at Collingwood is expected to know their football phrases. I was having a discussion with Shane Wakelin about game plans during preseason training. He was a big rap for zone defence whereas I said that I prefer a bit of man-on-man action. For some reason that floored him. He even asked me to repeat it. 'Sure,' I said. 'I prefer a bit of man-on-man action.' Wakes had a bit of a giggle. 'Have a good laugh,' I said. I know it's going back to the old days, but it's the only way to play accountable football. Wakes then suggested that if I felt so strongly about it, I should bring it up at the next players' meeting. 'I will,' I said. I'm more than happy to. I'm not embarrassed about it. So, there I am at the next team meeting, and Mick asks if anyone has any comments.

Wakes puts his hand up and says: 'Yep, Strauchanie's got something he confided in me the other day and now wants to tell the whole group.'

I proudly stood up and let my feelings be known. 'Mick, boys, there's something I've wanted to get off my chest. I hope you don't hold this against me, but I, Bryan Strauchan, am proud to announce that I prefer a bit of man-on-man action.'

Well, you could've heard a pin drop. And you would have, if Wakes wasn't giggling like a child for some reason. The fact of the matter is, that when it's in the last couple of minutes of the game, and the other team starts kicking the ball backwards in an effort to play for time, the only thing you can do is revert to man-on-man action. Sure, it's been a long game and you can't be bothered, but I can tell you, the crowds like nothing more than watching two hot, sweaty men going at it hell for leather. By the end of the meeting I think the boys had a clearer picture of where I was coming from. Except for Wakes. His laughing fit became so uncontrollable that he was forced to leave the room.

As Strauchanie's pointed out in the above example, whether you're a player, a coach or a supporter, being familiar with Australian Rules footballing jargon is vital. To avoid any confusion, and as a service to the football-going public, Strauchanie will now list and explain some football terminology. As you would be well aware, new words and phrases are introduced each year. Here are some of the newer ones, many of which Strauchanie himself has coined and uses personally.

strauchanievision: Only having eyes for the goals. Doesn't matter what's happening around you, your entire focus is on kicking the ball through the big sticks. Just because someone is in a better position doesn't necessarily mean they've got more chance of kicking the goal than Strauchanie. The price of bananas went up, but it didn't stop Strauchanie kicking them from the boundary. I've spent my career with coaches in my ear saying, 'Strauchanie, why do you keep having pings at goal from impossible angles?' I'd simply respond with, 'Superman had X-ray vision – superstars have strauchanievision'.

turdulence: When your team is going through a really rough patch during the year and opposition supporters are getting stuck into you, reassure yourself and the other followers of your team by saying, 'Sure, we may have lost a few games in a row, but we're just experiencing a bit of turdulence at the moment. Just fasten your seatbelts for now and we'll be through it shortly.' Carlton supporters have endured a turdulent five years.

the strauchanmower: When Strauchanie runs through you, you know you've been hit. Forget Byron Pickett. He's a poor Russian copy of the strauchanmower. The strauchanmower was a term first uttered by myself two years ago after

I mowed down three Under 12 boys when I was taking them for a training session. Bucks tries to claim that he coined the term when commenting on what was left of the food at a club function that I had arrived early to. 'Looks like the strauchanmower got to the food first,' alleged Bucks ... like he's quick enough to think of that on the spot!

Short-arse League: A proposal Strauchanie put forward to the AFL regarding the Little League. Instead of just kids playing in it, anyone under 5' 3" should be eligible to play. I mean, let's face it, the Little League is getting pretty boring, so what better way to spice it up than by throwing some angry short men in there? One of the best footballers Horsham ever produced, besides yours truly, was a dwarf by the name of Tommy Watkins. He was the Leigh Matthews of dwarves. Tough, skilful, uncompromising and one hell of a leader. He could kick around his body, kick over his head, or even kick himself in the head, especially if he was unhappy with a missed shot on goal. Now, there's a guy who would love the opportunity to run around on the G. Come on AFL, make it happen.

clangtastic: When you do a clanger on purpose, just to make the highlights reel. Can be a useful method of ensuring your noggin makes the TV that night, but be careful not to abuse it. Carlton got a bit carried away with it a couple of years ago. There must have been some sort of competition between the players that year because there was clangtastic footage from certain Carlton games that went for a solid 10 minutes.

strauchanicity: Having that 'it' quality. Only the most exceptional of footballers could expect to have the strauchanicity label attached to them. AFL recruiters have been known to rank prospective draft picks according to their strauchanicity. Bryce Gibbs was oozing strauchanicity. It's not something you can teach. You're either born with strauchnicity or you're not.

the pie eye punt: Any kick that goes into the crowd and knocks a pie out of someone's hands. If you nail a perfect pie eye punt, you'll knock the pie into the face of the guy trying to eat it. Another variation is the 'super pie eye punt', which involves a kick that knocks over the kid who walks around selling the pies. Alan Didak tried to claim a super pie eye punt last year until a close inspection of the replay on Fox Footy revealed that he'd hit the kid selling the ice-creams instead.

donstipation: When you shut Essendon down to the point where there is no movement at all. Quite a painful experience for Bomber fans. Can be a dangerous tactic because, when the movement eventually happens again, it all comes at once and you can be in all sorts of trouble.

vosstate check: When each club checks through its playing list to see how many Michael Voss types it has. Every club should have a 'vosstate check' on a regular basis to ensure that their list remains in a healthy condition. You need Michael Voss types coming through your system continually if you are to achieve sustained success. I'm sure that when Collingwood does its vosstate check, Strauchanie is the first name that pops up.

straupedo: A mongrel punt perfected by Strauchanie that is specifically designed to break the fingers of opposition players. Many have tried, but only Strauchanie has mastered the technique. I let my teammates know when I'm doing one, so that they can get out of the way. One Straupedo I did at Williamstown last year broke a player's fingers and then flew into the crowd knocking a guy's pie out of his hands. Officially becoming the first ever, crossbred, straupedo pie eye punt.

hedgesledging: This is sledging where you cover all your bases to ensure you don't miss anything. I'll give you an example. 'Yeah, you're no good! Well, that's what your girlfriend told me last night … or your boyfriend … whichever one applies … but yeah, she … or he … was all over me last night.'

rooseyliscious: Anything at all to do with Paul Roos. He's the man. Everything he touches, endorses or even looks at is rooseyliscious. The Swans premiership in 2005 was so rooseyliscious it wasn't funny. How do you think Ross Lyon got the job at St Kilda? They just wanted to suck as much rooseyliscious out of him as possible. Strauchanie certainly wouldn't mind a bit of rooseyliscious himself.

derminator: A player who goes hard during a game and goes equally as hard when out at a nightclub, not referring to anyone in particular. The term just came to Strauchanie when he was in an unconscious stupor, flaked out in the corner of a nightclub. That same night I may have been talking to an ex-champion of the game who just happened to have taken that particular nightclub by the scruff of the neck, shaking it to its very foundations.

strauchanberry fields: Footy grounds that have seen a match-winning display by Strauchanie. At last count there were about 145 strauchanberry fields on the list, each, at some stage, bearing witness to some Strauchanie magic. There is, of course, only one ground left to add to Strauchanie's list. Put it this way, it won't be long before people will be referring to the G as the SF – the big Strauchanberry Field.

weaglewired: Anyone who looks like they're under the influence of an illegal substance. Possible symptoms and side effects include winning a premiership and/or flatlining.

PAGE 154: 'weaglewired"

Bryan, for legal reasons, you must make it clear that no reference to any particular player, past or present, is intended in this statement.

No reference to any player ... blah, blah what publisher said (so don't sue me) – BS

CHAPTER FIFTEEN->

fifteen

I imagine that as you're reading this you are probably crying and thinking about calling your loved ones and telling them how much you love them and how much they mean to you. Strauchanie's story often has that emotional impact on people. By the time this book is published, I imagine I will have hit it big in the States. I may even be playing in the NFL. *My Story* is probably already on Oprah's Book Club just above *Tuesdays With Morrie*. Who knows, I may have even done a Zoot Review. It is my pleasure to be able to inspire, it's a gift, and God would want me to use it. We all have talents. Paul Licuria is good at making toast, Alan Didak is a reasonable driver and Josh Fraser can touch his nose with his tongue. All impressive talents that their parents would be proud of, yet they pale in comparison to the achievements of B.K. Strauchan. Strauchanie can light up lives with a smile, a specky or an autographed footy card. I have a way with people. Whereas some players don't like

South Sydney District Rugby League Football Club Limited
ABN. 28 002 487 390

Locked Bag 1 Redfern NSW 2016

Tel +61 2 8306 9900
Fax +61 2 8306 9911
Email thumper@souths.com.au
Web souths.com.au

25 June, 2007

Dear Bryan,

Thanks you for your letter and the unique opportunity you afforded our club. At this stage salary cap demands and remaining strands of sanity prevent us from taking you up on your offer of an immediate place in our first grade squad. I couldn't find any NRL reference on the players you listed as having made the "successful transition" between our codes.
I would point out though that Andrew Bogut is a basketball player, but yes he is indeed "a tall ****".

No doubt as you say, the price you quoted would indeed be a bargain for a talent such as yours, the team "hooker" though is not negotiable as an "out of the cap exclusive benefit" and fulfils a completely different role in our organization than you imagine. Has it occurred to you to watch a game? I know it comes on late down there, but I think you might find it instructive.

As you suggested, I called Eddie McGuire, he was, as you said he would be, "very keen" on you switching codes. Not however for the reasons you stated. You do indeed have a friend there, he talked very highly of how you talk yourself up and was sincere in saying you believe every word.

The information that you'd shot both magpies and rabbits as a child was colourful but it didn't lead our recruitment committee to your same conclusions. Maybe you are right, it is more "today/tonight" and could well backfire on you.

Thanks again for your letter.
Yours sincerely,

Russell Crowe

conversing with the fans, I am proud to say that I have slept with nine members of the cheer squad. Joffa even burst in one night wearing the gold jacket, just to let the young lass know it was 'Game Over'.

As I sit here in the locker room trying to block out Mick's voice as he addresses the playing group, I realise that what I have achieved is nothing less than miraculous. Born in Horsham, I was shunned by kids at school for my freakish ability with the footy and my Asian good looks. I fought racism, a peanut allergy and chronic chafing to become the greatest footballer since, well, ever. They tried to say I couldn't do it but who else has made his debut in a Legends game? People often ask me how I got to be so good. I think a lot of it has to do with my heritage. Or at least my upbringing. Strauchanie has the aerial grace of a martial arts expert crossed with the ability to throw a Horsham haymaker from behind when the time comes. Sure, there have been disappointments along the way: missing the Horsham 2001 Grand Final after blowing a head gasket in the KFC car park while waiting for my popcorn chicken rates pretty highly, but there have been so many highs, all of them natural, I might add. Every time I was down, I got up again. Like that time in Las Vegas where I flatlined. The staff at Taco Bell arrived just in time to revive Strauchanie. I said to the young teenagers who had gathered around that they hadn't just saved one life, they had saved an entire sport, an entire culture, an entire nation. Strauchanie will live to take speckies for another day and if you think Strauchanie's good now, just wait until he gets a game with the Pies ...

Strauchanie had his appendix out when he was 13! lol. Strauchanie!!

appendix

Strauchanie's All Asian Team of the Century

Strauchanie revealed his All Asian Team of The Century at his favourite Chinese restaurant in Horsham: Jimmy Wan-cando's 'Flying Ox'. Jimmy will take good care of you, especially if you drop Straucha-nie's name. As Jimmy says [albeit in broken English which gives the restaurant an authentic atmosphere] 'Wha-ever you want, Jimmy Wan-can-do!' He is famous around Horsham for his 'Wan-can-do' attitude. Even when the health inspectors closed him down after nine bandaids were found in his Mongolian beef stir-fry, he came back better than ever. It was a wonderful night despite a lower than expected attendance

APPENDIX

[there were 12 people, we catered for 300]. It did nothing to dampen the occasion though with Strauchanie doing a top job as the emcee, firing off the night with a twenty-five minute monologue that had everything from hot topical gags [Strauchanie let rip on the banks and Lindy Chamberlain] and impressions [have you ever wondered what Andrew Demetriou would sound like if *he* was Asian?]. The band Strauchanie hired rocked the place too, a local band that combined Asian culture with hip-hop, the Bling Dynasty are bound for big things and Strauchanie tips that 'Terracotta Biatch', 'Number 27 With Fry Rice' and the emotional power ballad 'The Great Wall Around My Heart' will be chart toppers by the end of the year. Unfortunately they charge like a wounded bull in a Chinese restaurant and, as a result, it looks like Jimmy will have to close down again to pay the band. I am sure he will be back because, as everyone down Horsham way knows, Jimmy has that Wan-can-do attitude!

B	SEDAT SIR	MAL MICHAEL	ROY POY
HB	RON WEE HEE	DANNIE SEOW	TREV O'HOY
C	LES KEW MING	BRYAN STRAUCHAN	DAVID RODAN
HF	BACHAR HOULI	WALLY KOOCHEW	SUDJAI COOK
F	LES FONG	SAM PANG	WALLY KOOCHEW jnr

FOLLOWERS
NEALE FONG, PETER BELL, CAMERON LING

INTERCHANGE
ROY STRAUCHAN, TOMI JOHNSTON, AARON EDWARDS, GAVIN POY

PLAYER PROFILES

LES FONG Brilliant at ground level, this Dennis Cometti-coached forward played 284 games for West Perth. Was famous for his chopstick tricks at players' revues. One of China's best.

MAL MICHAEL This Papua New Guinea triple premiership player from the Lions is the third biggest celebrity in PNG behind the nation's first Prime Minister Michael Thomas Somare, and Wawa.

ROY POY From the province of Guangzhou but based in Albury where he played under Murray Weideman. Retired to help his dad out as a bookmaker. He once took a bet on Strauchanie to kick 13 goals plus in a semifinal against Bairnsdale. Strauchanie kicked 2.17 that day. Roy Poy was full of Roy Joy that day!

RON WEE HEE The Bendigo-based Chinese Dragon from the 1950s was hard at a contest and introduced the idea of feng shui into Australian football, once placing a lamp shade over a point post.

DANNIE SEOW Dannie played for Collingwood and Melbourne from 1986–90. He left to train as a wide receiver in America, but has since returned to Shanghai. In Strauchanie's eyes, wasted talent.

APPENDIX

TREVOR O'HOY Rated by Bucks as the best Chinese player he has seen outside Strauchanie. Played for St Kilda in 1973 and came runner up in the Gardiner Medal. An old-fashioned utility player who is now a head of Foster's [as in job-wise, not the frothy bit at the top of Foster's].

LES KEW MING Les played at North Melbourne in the 1920s and got the town talking with a monster 73-yard drop-kick. There was a campaign to change Year of the Dog to Year of the Les. It sadly fell on deaf ears.

BRYAN STRAUCHAN [captain] Superstar of the game, icon of the competition, ambassador to the country. Strauchanie has proved himself time after time and is the greatest player ever to have walked onto an AFL ground. He kicks goals like the emperor kicks off his slippers. Simply, the greatest. *Bryan, you still haven't played a single game for Collingwood.*

DAVID RODAN From Fiji, which Strauchanie decided after a couple of lagers makes him 'Asian enough'. Little battler who was dropped by the Tigers only to be picked up by the Power and keeps on keeping on.

BACHAR HOULI The first devout Muslim to play Aussie Rules at the highest level was picked by the Bombers causing unnecessary concern in his community after an initial misunderstanding. He is an exciting prospect and sells almost as many badges as Strauchanie does! Potential superstar.

Did not my starring role in the Legends game take place on an AFL ground? So it's Mick's loss that Strauchanie hasn't played for the Pies.

WALLY KOOCHEW Wally Koochew is perhaps regarded by many as the second greatest, after Strauchanie, to pull on a footy jumper. Son of a Chinese immigrant who arrived from Whampoa from the Guangdong Province, playing four games for Carlton in 1908.

SUDJAI COOK Seven games for Norwood and three for the Adelaide Crows, he was denied his chance after some credible performances, one in particular at the Gabba. Was it racism? What's that, Strauchanie? A can of worms? Clink! Consider it open!

SEDAT SIR The Turkish Delight played a bit for the Western Bulldogs and had good hands and even better hair.

SAM PANG Proud Chinese footballer who played Under 19s for Collingwood but couldn't break into the seniors. Got to feel sorry for a bloke who doesn't get a chance at the big time, don't you? Poor bloke. Works in radio now and is considering a move to south-east Asia, Adrian Cronauer style! 'Good Morning, Hanoi!' Strauchanie loves that film.

WALLY KOOCHEW jnr Played for Melbourne before becoming Northcote's youngest ever playing coach. He had the skill of his dad with the good looks of another famous Junior: Freddie Prinze.

NEALE FONG Brother of Les, Dr Neale Fong played 12 WAFL games and is now involved with the West Coast

APPENDIX

Eagles as their chaplain, which obviously keeps him extremely busy.

PETER BELL [vice-captain] Ring a ding ding! Little Freo motor who just doesn't stop. The Korean missile is a testament to believing in yourself. I feel bad that Chris Connolly would trade Belly for Strauchanie quicker than you can say 'hello moto'.

CAMERON LING Good to have an Asian Fanta Pants in the team. Boosts morale with his sense of humour and red hair. Probably has ginger pubes, which is always funny come shower time.

ROY STRAUCHAN Father of Bryan. What's the opposite of pedigree because this bloke has it in spades!

TOMI JOHNSTON Young gun on the rise. Strauchanie likes the look of him, a black belt in kicking arse and hardball gets.

AARON EDWARDS Samoan who has grabbed his chance at the Kangas like Mum grabbing a microphone at karaoke night.

GAVIN POY The tallest of the Poys who rucks for Lavington in the Murray and Ovens league. An Asian in the ruck? Boy, we have come a long way!

bibliography

Strauchanie's time is precious and so is yours so I'm saving you time and giving you a list of books I wouldn't bother with if I was you. I have seen Jimmy Clement reading proper books but he's complicated (see page 38).

Akermanis, Jason, *AKA: The battle within*, GSP, 2004
What about the battle the Pies will have WITHOUT Strauchanie???? Read Chapter 12 of my book instead.

Blume, Judy, *Are You There God? It's Me, Margaret*, Atheneum/Richard Jackson Books, 2001
One of the most emotional things Strauchanie has ever read ... Made me cry ... But in a tough way.

Buckley, Nathan, *My Story*
Not published yet but he's bound to jump on Strauchanie's bandwagon with the title and will probably beg me to do his foreword.

Cometti, Dennis, *That's Ambitious*, Allen & Unwin, 2007
Ha ha. Cometti doing a book. That IS ambitious! What's his claim to fame? Actually, the publisher made me include this but compared to the other books it's not that bad. Not many words.

BIBLIOGRAPHY
Bryan, since you have not provided footnotes (or in many cases any evidence at all) to support your facts, please provide a list of all the books you used for your research to be included in a bibliography.

Corby, Schapelle, *My Story,* Pan Macmillan, 2006
Copy cat. Read my email on page 78 instead.

Eastman, P.D., *Are you my mother?* Random House,
first published 1960
Too sad for Strauchanie in light of the revelations in Chapter 8. But if the adoption thing sells books, could be Strauchanie's next title.

Hird, James and Wilmoth. P, *Reading the play: On life and leadership.* Pan Macmillan, 2006
It's not play, it's hard work! (Something Hirdy would know all about if he'd had to write a book all by himself.) And 2006 – Ancient history!

Icons of Australian Sport: Leigh Matthews
Don't bother. Wait till *Icons of Australian Sport: Bryan Strauchan.* Soy Bean has kept all Strauchanie's stuff for when this mob come knocking.

Lewis, Michael, *Moneyball,* W. W. Norton & Company, 2004
Ha ha! Is this Tyson Goldsack's book?

Lyon, Garry and Arena, Felice:
   Specky Magee & the Boots of Glory
   Specky Magee & The Great Footy Contest
   Specky Magee & the Season of Champions
   Specky Magee and a Legend in the Making
   Specky Magee and the Spirit of the Game
Just change Specky Magee to Strauchanie and then you'll have some bestsellers on your hands, Garry Lyon! But Strauchanie would need a big slice of the pie if you use his name.

   Actually Garry, call me if you are interested in discussing this idea further.

Powers, John, *The Coach: A Season with Ron Barassi*, GSP, 2005 (originally published in 1978)
Even more ancient history! Wait for Strauchanie's next book: *A Season with Strauchanie!*

Watson, Tim, *Kevin Sheedy: The Jigsaw Man*, Pan Macmillan, 2006
It hasn't got a single jigsaw in it. Strauchanie was expecting puzzles. Where's the sodoku, Sheeds?

acknowledgements

BRYAN STRAUCHAN
Bryan Strauchan would like to thank Tiger Woods, Roger Federer and Makybe Diva for joining him in his pursuit of sporting excellence.

PETER HELLIAR
A huge thank you to the Collingwood Football Club for allowing unprecedented access to your facilities and players. I am living the dream every time I walk into that place. To the playing group, thanks for appearing in the filmed segments, putting up with me and a camera crew, and understanding that sometimes we have to turn music/TVs/Playstations down to shoot stuff. To Nicki Malady, huge thanks for facilitating all of this, you are the best in the business. To Balmey and Greg Swan [Strauchanie misses you both!], thanks for meeting us for a coffee three-and-a-half years ago and thinking that maybe allowing me to wear a Collingwood tracksuit and hang around the club was not the worst idea in the world. To Brodie and Sarita, thanks for letting us film in your home. To Maxy Kleiman, thanks for always being camera ready [Strauchanie misses you too mate!]. To Mick Malthouse for being extremely welcoming and *not* the scary person he is supposed to be [and for letting Strauchanie date your daughter!]. To Christi, thanks so much for agreeing to be part of Strauchanie's life before anyone could know if it was going to end up in tears or not! To Eddie, thanks for encouraging the idea. The list goes on at the great club: Eugene Arocca, Anthony Trainor, the girls at reception [we occasionally shove a camera in their faces and say 'Just pretend Strauchanie has …'], Bucks, Lica, Dids, Wakes, Pebs, Dale, Brad Dick, Harry for being most prepared to jump in front of a camera. No doubt I have forgotten people but to everyone in that joint, massive thanks.

To all the players/coaches from the 15 other clubs who have appeared with or embraced Strauchanie – thanks for being a huge part of it!

To the fans that have soaked up Strauchanie to sometimes dangerous levels, thank you. The reaction to Strauchanie has been overwhelming.

BRYAN STRAUCHAN: MY STORY

Thanks to everyone at Channel 10 who backs Strauchanie and *Before The Game*: David Mott, Kerry Kingston, David White, Sam Heard, Peter Andrews and Stephanie Bansemer-Brown.

Thanks to my family on *Before The Game*: Hughesy, Lehmo, Sam, and Andy. It's criminal how easy this show is to do!!! Couldn't think of a better way to spend Saturday afternoons [just don't tell my wife, she thinks I'm working!]. To Michelle Wyatt for your unwavering faith and for putting so much time and effort into BS! Here's looking at you Shannon 'Scrapper' Davis, Adrian Brown, Aimz, Quarters, Huddo, Vossy. JT – the best Tool Man in showbiz! Michael Chamberlin, Adam Rozenbachs – very, very funny men. Paul Walsh, Luke McManus, Haydos, Darren Lee, Mark, Sascha, Jacqui and all the make-up girls, Leticia ... again, everyone who makes that show get to air. Rove McManus and Craig Campbell and all at Roving Enterprises: thanks. And to Kevin Whyte, Kathleen McCarthy, Dioni Meliss and all at Token Artists, more thanks. To Ma and Pa Strauchan [Margaret Chong and Frank Wyatt] for helping raise Strauchanie.

To my publisher at Allen & Unwin, Andrea McNamara, and Pauline Haas – this book is so much better because you jumped in headfirst and came up with some inspired stuff ... you can write with us anytime!! And to Dan Warner for the commas, the spelling, and so on. Thanks to John Harms and Sam Pang for the All Asian Team of the Century.

My actual family. Happiness is seeing my two boys, Liam and Aidan, in Collingwood jumpers playing kick to kick together. Brij, thanks for putting up with me watching way too much football and for not having me around on Saturdays [... but it's bloody hard work this!] Mum, Dad, Mark, Karen, Rachel, Rowdy and Lisa – thanks for handling questions and ticket requests.

And finally, massive thanks to my co-author and co-creator Mr Paul Calleja [no, not the guy who plays for the Crows]. We've been mates for years now and you know how highly I rate you. Thank you for walking into the boardroom one day and saying, 'I reckon Pete should play a character who plays for Collingwood ...' It's been an amazing ride. You are an out-and-out champion.

How come you gave <u>him</u> so much space here?!?

ACKNOWLEDGEMENTS

PAUL CALLEJA

Thanks to the three girls I live with – Michelle, Marlowe and Roxy – for their ongoing support and genuine interest; to Pat and Richard Calleja, who taught me so much about all sorts of things; to the *Before the Game* cast and staff who do a sensational job and have become my extended family; and to Adam Rozenbachs for his creative contributions to the Strauchanie story. To Peter Helliar for his friendship and ability to make me laugh. And finally, to Strauchanie, for having an ego the size of the MCG and yet still managing to capture the hearts of football fans around the world.

PHOTOGRAPHIC CREDITS

1. Me, since that's who they're all of

All portraits of Bryan Strauchan used in chapter openers and throughout, except where mentioned below, were taken by James Penlidis.

Photos of young Strauchanie are from the author's private collection (also taken by James Penlidis).

The stills on pages xiv, 24, 36, 45, 58, 61, 70, 86, 98, 100, 105, 129, 130, 133, 142 and 160 are from *Before the Game* and are used courtesy of Roving Enterprises (and the subjects). As if they'd say NO to being in Strauchanie's book!

Colour picture section:

Page 1: Footy card courtesy of Select.

Page 2 (top): Courtesy of Getty images.

Page 2 (bottom): Courtesy of Roving Enterprises (and Bucks, Jimmy and Mick).

Page 3: Strauchanie's superskills were captured by James Penlidis

Page 4: Courtesy of GSP Images; photographer Lachlan Cunningham.

What's with the courtesy thing? Why so polite? Relax — it's for Strauchanie!

index

Strauchanie has included lots of names in the index because that's what people look up to see if they're in the book.

Aka (aka 'Jason Akermanis') 55
All Asian Team of the Century 160–5
Anthony, Jack (aka 'JA') 39
Asia *see* whole book because it would be racist to leave some page numbers out

Bacardi Breezer *see* Lloydy
B-caf (aka 'Brent Macaffer') 52
Bean, Soy (aka 'Mum') *see also* lemon chicken, xv, all of Chapter 2, 86–7,
Bell, Peter 108
Bentley, Mark 29
BFG 46 *see also* Pebbles
birth of Strauchanie 22 *see also* Chapter 8
bonus (what Hirdy's book has none of), too many to list so find them yourself
Bracksie (aka 'Steve Bracks' or 'The Honourable') 99
Brown, Nathan (dime a dozen) 41
Brownlow Café 126, 131
Brownlow xvi, 4, 40, 46, 67, 97, 117, 125, 132, 134, 146
Bryan, Chris (who needs to change his name because there's only one Bryan) 50
Bucks (aka 'Nathan Buckley' or 'Buckanara' or 'Buck Nathanley') xiii, 37, 41, 44, 47, 51, 97, 118, 131, 151, 163, all of Chapter 6
Burns, Scott 44, 99

Carpet Burn Fake Grass Pty Ltd 140–1
Chef, the (aka Ryan Cook) 47
champion *see* Strauchan, Bryan
chicken, lemon, recipe (a Strauchanie bonus!) 20, 135
Choco (aka 'Mark Williams') 133

Churchill, Winston 67
Clarke, Martin (who should not get a game before Stracuanie!) 52
Clement, James (Strauchanie's number one fan) xiii, 38, 45, 47, 69, 166,
Cloke, Travis 39, 48
Collingwood Football Club xvii, 55, 61 and lots more; read it yourself
Committee, Rules 72
Connolly, Chris 129
Cook, Sudjai 164
copycat 7, 9, 44, 46, 94
Corbs (aka 'Schapelle Corby') 78–9
Cox, Shannon 40 *see also* grow up
Crawford, Shane 130–1
Croatia *see* Didak, Alan

Dad *see* Strauchan, Roy (and you had probably better read Chapter 8 too)
Daniher, Neale 132
Davies, Ben 44 *see also* copycat
Davis, Leon (aka 'Neon') 36, 99, 110
Dawes, Chris 48
Daylesford *see* lesbian
Demetriou, Andrew 106
Dick, Brad (what were his parents thinking?) 39, 48 *see also* grow up
Dids (aka 'Alan Didak') 37, 109, 140, 156 *see also* Croatia
Dynasty, Han 18
Dyson, Craig (included because of role in Fratelli, Linda story) 29

Eade, Rocket (aka 'Blast Off') 135
Eddie *see* McGuire
Edwards, Aaron 165

INDEX

Egan, Chris 41, 67, 99
Fong, Les 162
Fong, Neale 164
Fowler, Dylan 59
Fowler, Gary 59 (Strauchanie!)
Fraser, Josh 46, 67, 156
Fratelli, Linda 29–34

Goldsack, Tyson 50 *see also* grow up
Goodsey (aka 'Adam Goodes') 116–7, 122
Grandfather (this is on the Asian side) 16, all of Chapter 2
Grandma *see* Strauchan, Betty
Grandmother (this is on the Asian side) 17, all of Chapter 2
grow up (advice to Collingwood selectors) 40
Guy, the Tall (aka 'Guy Richards') 45

Hahn, Mitch (no relation) 18
hair *see* Medhurst, Thomas, Iles, Burns, Lockyer and Strauchanieeeee!
Harmsey (Wayne, not the writer guy) 55
Hird, James (aka 'James Hird "All-About-It"' or 'Hirdy') xiv, 21, 88, 94, 96, 127
history, Australian (don't worry about what they teach you in school, just read Chapters 1 and 2 because all the big stuff is covered)
history, rewriting (to get better ending) 55
Holland, Brodie 38, 98, 109
Horsham 19, 90, all of Chapter 11 *see also* Strauchan, Roy
Houli, Bachar 163
Hoxley, umpire 89–91

Iles, Sam 50
injured *see* (at time of going to press) Rusling, Bucks, Presti, 'Yeah I'm' Shaw, the Wax, JA (so you would think Mick would be giving Strauchanie a game)
Jeans, Yabby 54
Jenkins, Jerker 55
Johnson, Ben 46, 95, 97, 99

Johnson, Tomi 164
Jolie, Angelina 86
Jolie-Pitt, Maddox 86

Kane, Clancy *see* history, Australian (not sure if he's related to the Overflow guy)
Kelly *see* Ned, Paul, Craig, Dame Kelly Melba (too many to list the pages)
Kew Ming, Les 163
Knife, Stanley (aka 'Danny Stanley') 47
Koochew, Wally and Wally jnr 164
Koschitzke, Justin 55

lesbian *see* Strauchan, Betty
Lexus (the only car they let me mention)
Lica (aka 'Paul Licuria') 28, 47, 81, 98, 107, 113, 143 *see also* Spanish trivia nights
Ling, Cameron 161 *see also* joke 97
Lloyd, Matthew (aka 'Matty' or 'Lloydy') 70, 76–83, 127 *see also* Bacardi Breezer
Lock-it-in (aka 'Tarkyn Lockyer') 46, 59, 67
Lonie, Ryan 37, 95

Malthouse, Christi xvi, 62, all of Chapter 10
Malthouse, Mick xiv, 61–4, 104, 105, 136, 140, 158
Mandela, Nelson 67, 117
man-vorce 46
Marlowe, Roxy 26 (only included because she's the type who would check)
Matthews, Leigh 151
mayor *see* Horsham or So, John depending on which one you want
McDonald's 77
McGuire, Eddie, all of Chapter 9
McLean, Brock 132
McLeod, Andrew 125
Medibank (aka 'Paul Medhurst') 38 *see also* hair
Michael, Mal 162
Mum *see* Bean, Soy (and you had probably better read Chapter 8 too)

Nicholson, Jack 89

173

BRYAN STRAUCHAN: MY STORY

Norman, Robert Harvey (aka 'Robert Harvey') 134

O'Hoy, Trevor 163

Pang, Sam 164
Pebbles (aka Anthony Rocca) 46, 52, 55, 107, 142 *see also* BFG
pedigree, football, Strauchanie's xv,
Pendles (aka Scott Pendlebury) 39, 95
Phillips, Betty *see* Grandma
Pickett, Byron 150
Pickles, Danny (aka 'Danny Nicholls') 52
Plugger 107
Poy, Gavin 165
Poy, Roy 162
Presti (aka Simon Prestigiacomo) 48, 99
publisher (too many @#%&* mentions!)

Quigley, Lawrence *see* Lloyd, Matthew

Reid, Ben (aka MS Readathon) 45
Ricciuto, Mark *see* scurvy
Richards (this is like Brown and Kelly, too many of them)
Roberton, Russell 132
Rodan, David 163
Rusling, Sean 37, 84 *see also* injured

sausages 54
school 24–34
Schwarze, Troy 134
scurvy 125
Seow, Dannie 162
Shaw, 'R U' (aka 'Heath Shaw') 50, 69, 81
Shaw, 'Yeah I'm' (aka 'Rhyce Shaw') 45, 69, 143
Sir, Sedat 164
skill, football *see* Strauchan, Bryan 'Superstar'
Skilton, Bobby xiv–v
sledge 13
Smart, Maxwell (aka 'Nick Maxwell' or 'Max Nickwell') 46, 59

Smorgy's 95
So, John 91
Spanish trivia nights *see* Licuria, Paul
Stella, Sarita (no page numbers given because BH gets jealous)
Strauchan, Betty (aka 'Grandma Betty' and 'Nanna Betty') 3, all of Chapter 1
Strauchan, Bryan Keith (aka 'Strauchanie' and 'BS') *see* the whole book
Strauchan, Ernest (aka 'Grandad Ernest') 3, all of Chapter 1
Strauchan, Roy (aka 'Dad') xv, xv, all of Chapter 1, 165
Strauchanie, the Big 119–22
superstar *see* Strauchan, Bryan
Swan, Dane 50, 99, 100, 113–4
Swann, Greg 100

talent *see* Strauchan, Bryan and Malthouse, Christi
teams, other than Collingwood 123–36
Temptation 68 see also Malthouse, Christi and Fratelli, Linda
Thomas, Dale 7, 40, 99, 100
Thompson, Archie 139
Thorpedo 42
Toovey, Alan 48
Train, Davey (aka 'Aaron Davey') 132

Voss, Michael 126, 152

Wakes (aka 'Shane Wakelin') 14, 41, 149
Wan, Obi (aka 'Shane O'Bree') 40, 81
Wax, the (aka 'Harry O'Brien' or 'the Boy from Brazil') 47, 99, 138
Wee Hee, Ron 162
weird cult *see* Wellingham, Sharrod
Wellingham, Sharrod 52 *see also* weird cult
Williams, Mark 55

adoption 86–92 (out of order but wouldn't want to give the story away by putting it first)